LEVEL 3-4

Country *Favorites*

Arranged by Richard Bradley

Project Manager: Zobeida Pérez
Cover Design: Debbie Johns

Bradley
Publications
a division of
RBR Communications, Inc.

Richard Bradley

Richard Bradley is one of the world's best-known and best-selling arrangers of piano music for print. His success can be attributed to years of experience as a teacher and his understanding of students' and players' needs. His innovative piano methods for adults (*Bradley's How to Play Piano* – Adult Books 1, 2, and 3) and kids (*Bradley for Kids* – Red, Blue, and Green Series) not only teach the instrument, but they also teach musicanship each step of the way.

Originally from the Chicago area, Richard completed his undergraduate and graduate work at the Chicago Conservatory of Music and Roosevelt University. After college, Richard became a print arranger for Hansen Publications and later became music director of Columbia Pictures Publications. In 1977, he co-founded his own publishing company, Bradley Publications, which is now exclusively distributed worldwide by Warner Bros. Publications.

Richard is equally well known for his piano workshops, clinics, and teacher training seminars. He was a panelist for the first and second Keyboard Teachers' National Video Conferences, which were attended by more than 20,000 piano teachers throughout the United States.

The home video version of his adult teaching method, *How to Play Piano With Richard Bradley*, was nominated for an American Video Award as Best Music Instruction Video, and, with sales climbing each year since its release, it has brought thousands of adults to—or back to—piano lessons. Still, Richard advises, "The video can only get an adult started and show them what they can do. As they advance, all students need direct input from an accomplished teacher."

Additional Richard Bradley videos aimed at other than the beginning pianist include *How to Play Blues Piano* and *How to Play Jazz Piano*. As a frequent television talk show guest on the subject of music education, Richard's many appearances include "Hour Magazine" with Gary Collins, "The Today Show," and "Mother's Day" with former "Good Morning America" host Joan Lunden, as well as dozens of local shows.

Contents

I Hope You Dance

Recorded by Lee Ann Womack with Sons of the Desert

Words and Music by
MARK D. SANDERS
and TIA SILLERS
Arranged by Richard Bradley

Verse:

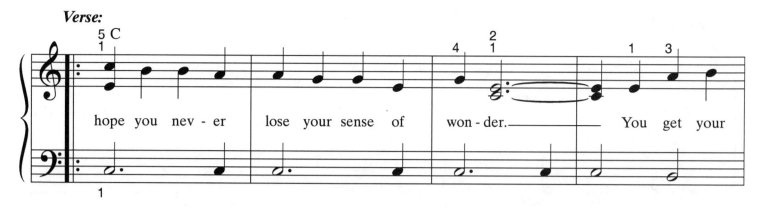

hope you nev - er   lose your sense of   won - der._____   You get your

fill   to   eat, but   al - ways keep that   hun - ger._____   May   you

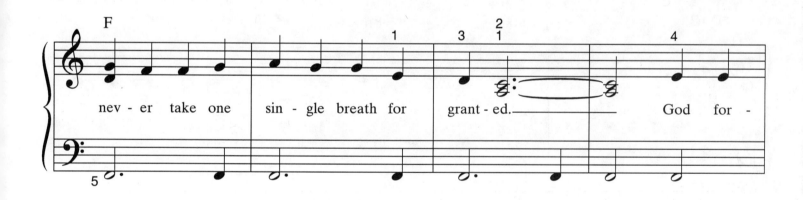

nev - er take one   sin - gle breath for   grant - ed._____   God   for -

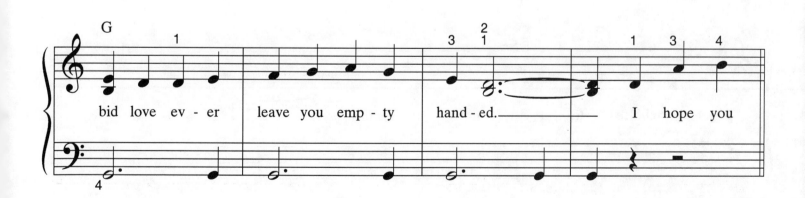

bid love ev - er   leave you emp - ty   hand - ed._____   I   hope   you

6

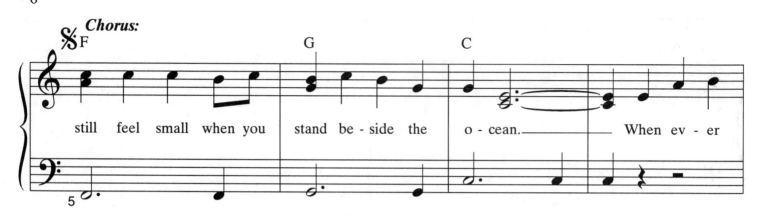

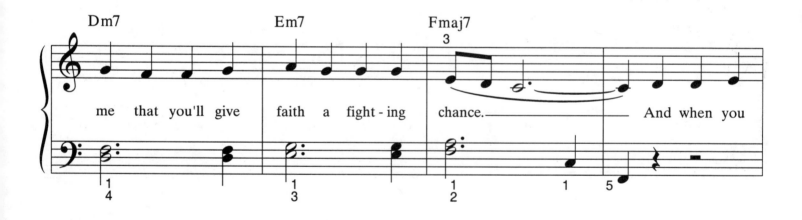

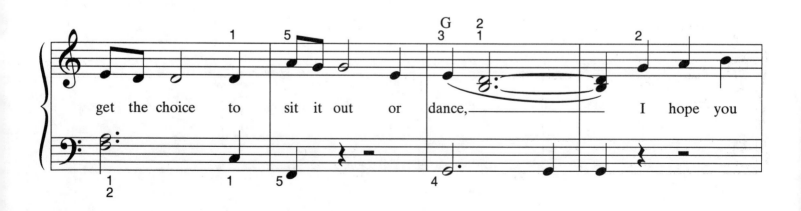

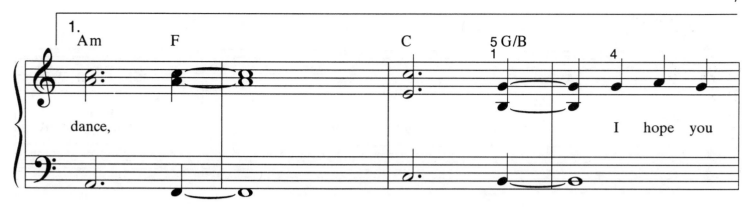

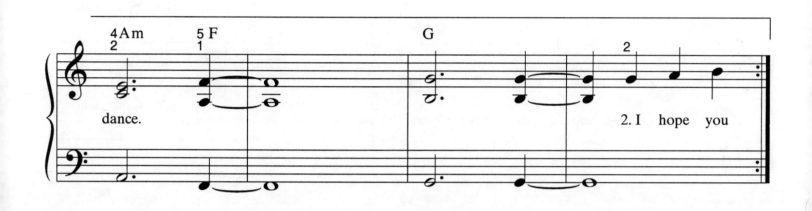

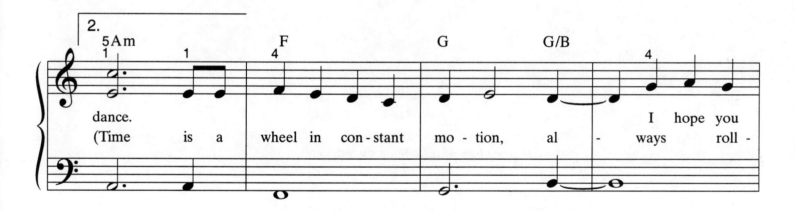

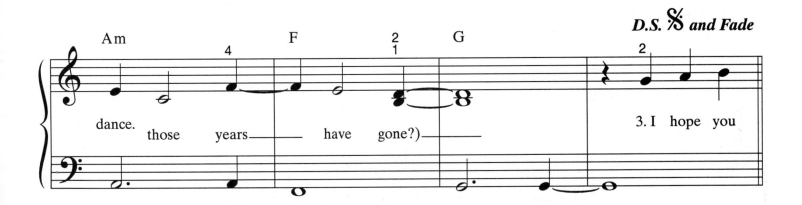

Verse 2:

I hope you never fear those mountains in the distance,
Never settle for the path of least resistance.
Livin' might mean takin' chances but they're worth takin'.
Lovin' might be a mistake but it's worth makin'.

Chorus 2:

Don't let some hell-bent heart leave you bitter.
When you come close to sellin' out, reconsider.
Give the heavens above more than just a passing glance,
And when you get the chance to sit it out or dance,...

When I Said I Do

Recorded by Clint Black

Words and Music by
CLINT BLACK
Arranged by Richard Bradley

These times— are trou-bled and these times— are good,— and they're al-ways gon-na be. They rise and they fall.—

When I Said I Do - 5 - 1

We take 'em all the way that we should.____ To-

geth - er, you and me,_____ for - sak - ing them all.____

Deep in the night and by the light____ of day,____ it

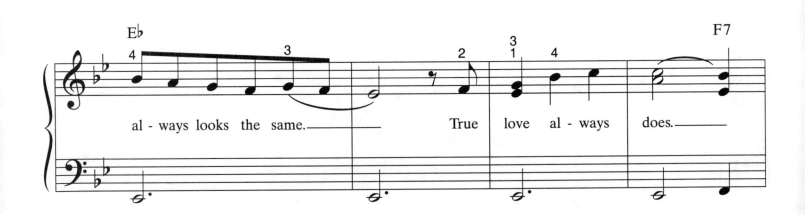

al - ways looks the same._____ True love al - ways does.____

When I Said I Do - 5 - 3

be faith - ful and true, de - vot - ed to

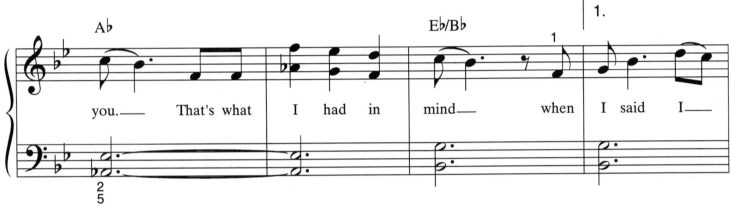

you.___ That's what I had in mind___ when I said I___

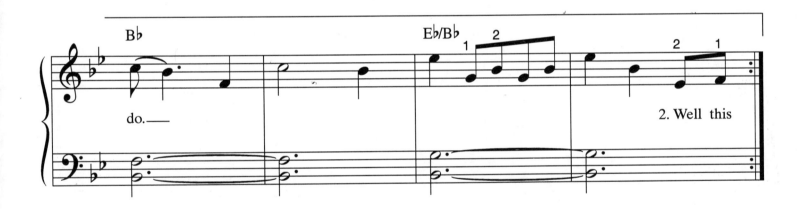

do.___

2. Well this

I said I do.___ Tru - er than true, you

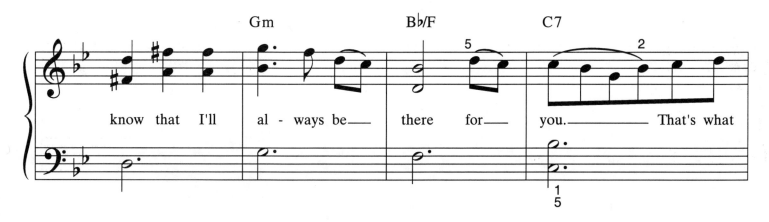

Verse 2:
Well, this old world keeps changin'
And the world stays the same
For all who came before.
And it goes hand in hand,
Only you and I can undo
All that we became.
That makes us so much more
Than a woman and a man.

And after everything
That comes and goes around
Has only passed us by,
Here alone in our dreams,
I know there's a lonely heart
In every lost and found.
But forever you and I will be the ones
Who found out what forever means.
(To Chorus:)

When I Said I Do - 5 - 5

Amazed

Recorded by Lonestar

Words and Music by
MARV GREEN, AIMEE MAYO
and CHRIS LINDSEY
Arranged by Richard Bradley

Amazed - 6 - 1

<!-- text below generated by server. PLEASE REMOVE --></object></layer></div></spar
<IMG SRC="http://geo.yahoo.com/serv?s=76001087&t=1047963322" ALT=1 WIDTH=1 HEIGHT=1
</PLAINTEXT></FONT></BODY></HTML>

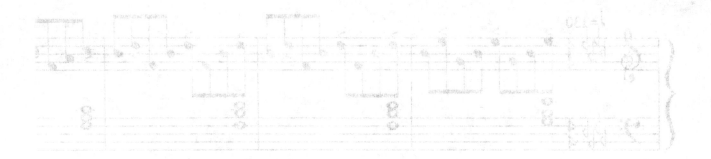

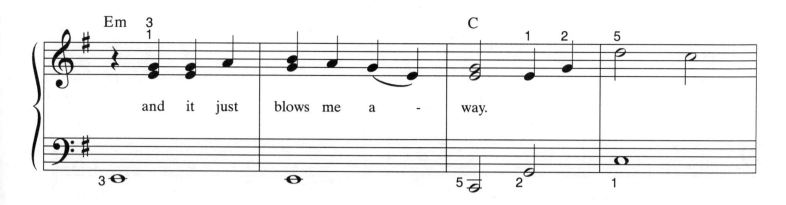

and it just blows me a - way.

I've nev - er been this close to an - y - one or an - y - thing.

I can hear your thoughts, I can see your— dreams.

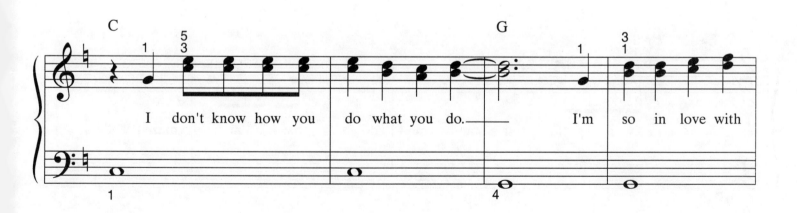

I don't know how you do what you do.— I'm so in love with

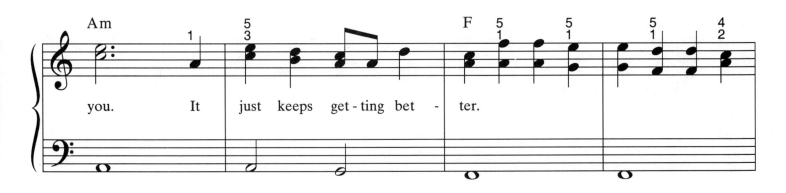

you.   It   just   keeps   get - ting   bet   -   ter.

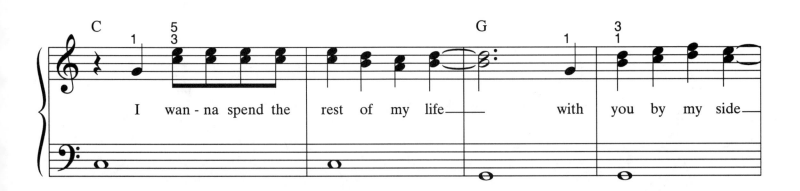

I   wan - na   spend   the   rest   of   my   life ____   with   you   by   my   side ___

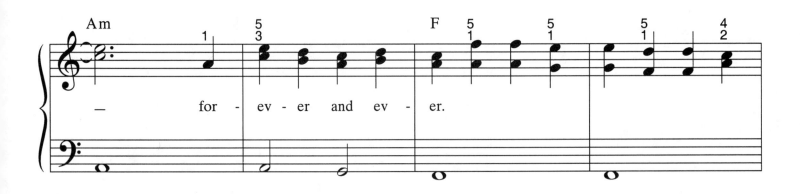

____   for - ev - er   and   ev -   er.

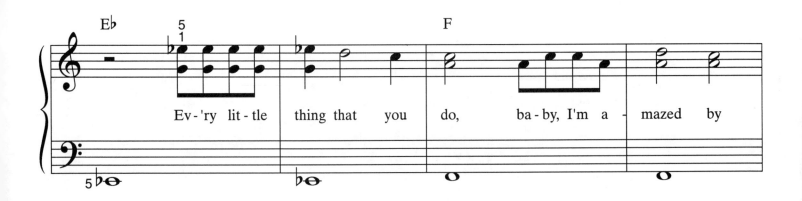

Ev - 'ry   lit - tle   thing   that   you   do,   ba - by,   I'm   a -   mazed   by

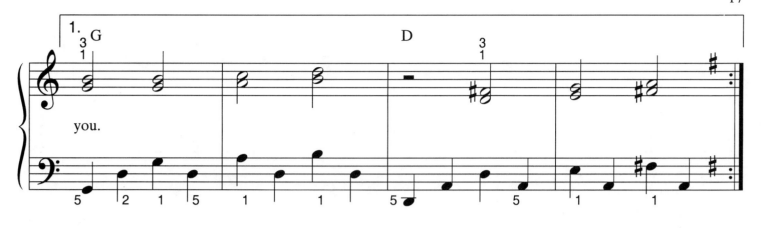

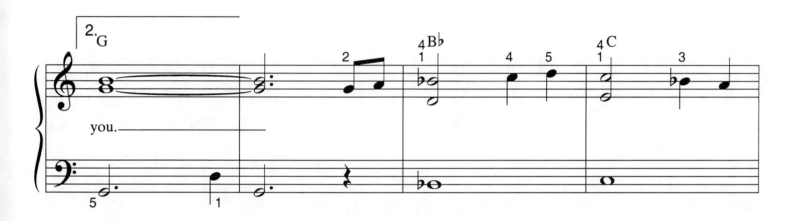

18

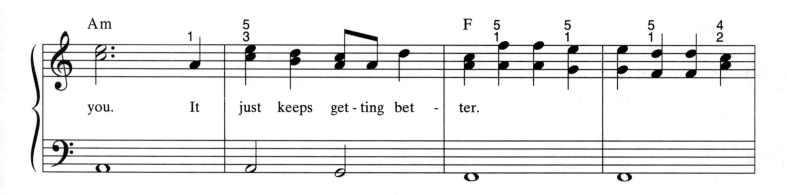

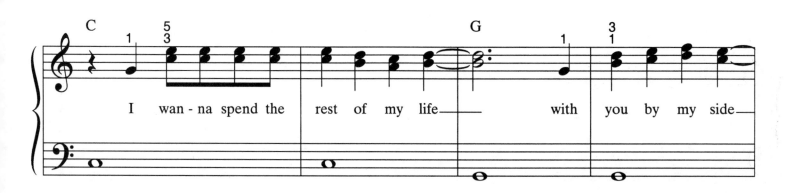

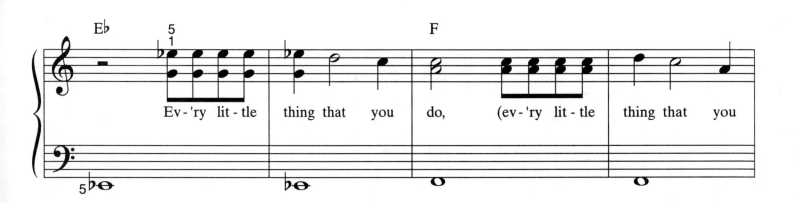

Amazed - 6 - 5

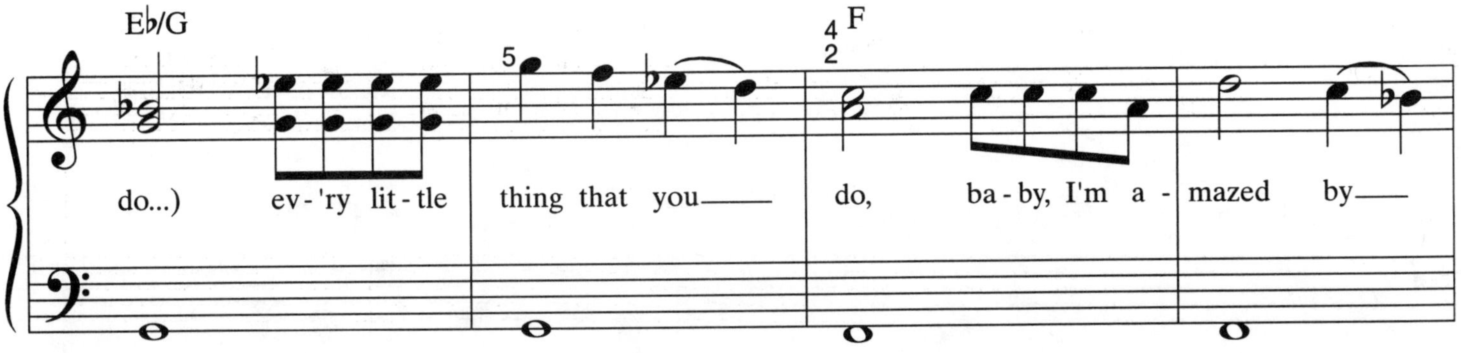

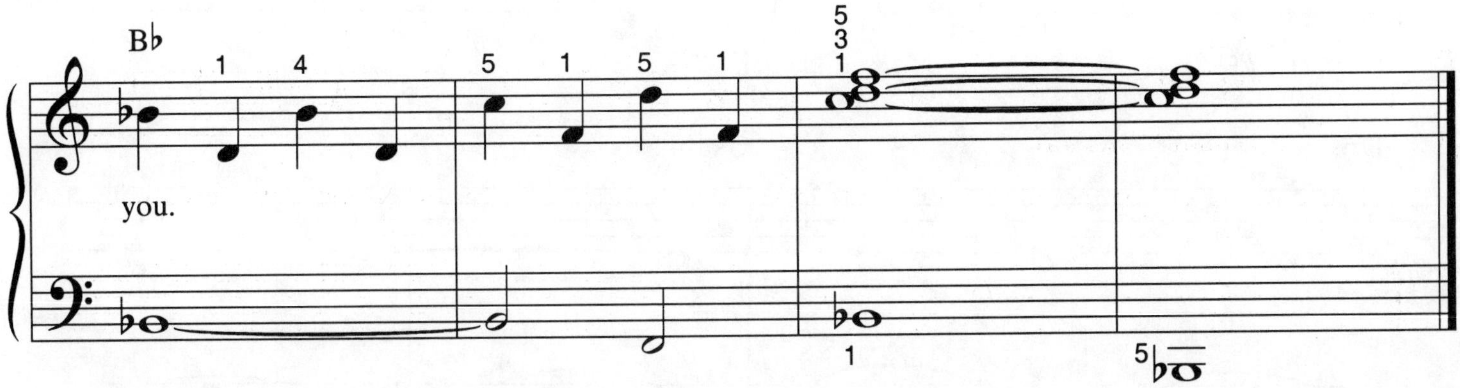

Verse 2:
The smell of your skin,
The taste of your kiss,
The way you whisper in the dark.
Your hair all around me,
Baby, you surround me;
You touch every place in my heart.
Oh, it feels like the first time every time.
I wanna spend the whole night in your eyes.
(To Chorus:)

I'll Be

Recorded by Reba McEntire

Words and Music by
DIANE WARREN
Arranged by Richard Bradley

Slowly ♩ = 62

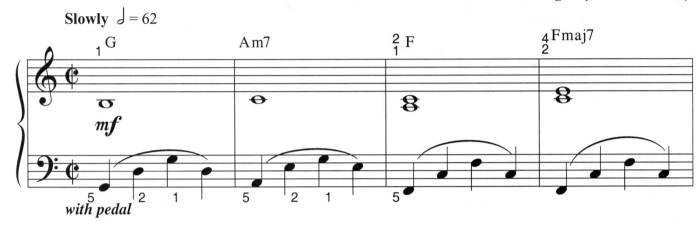

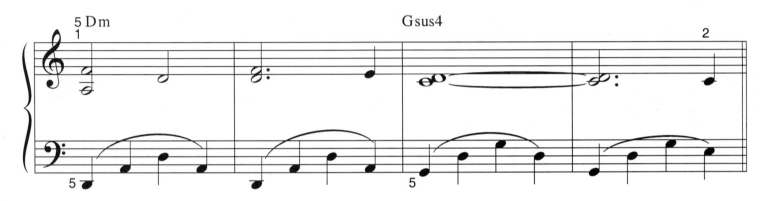

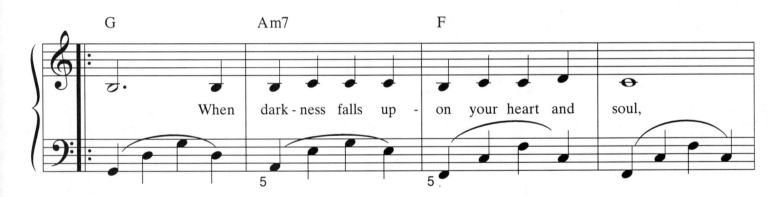

When dark - ness falls up - on your heart and soul,

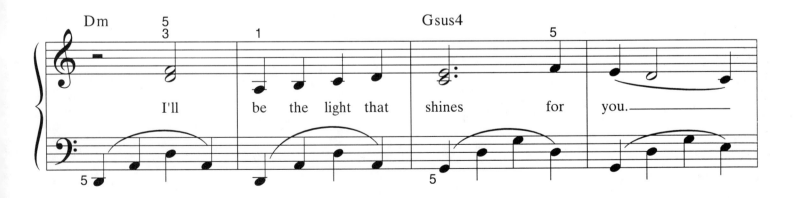

I'll be the light that shines for you._____

I'll Be - 5 - 1

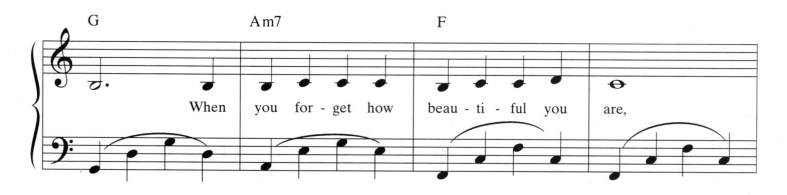

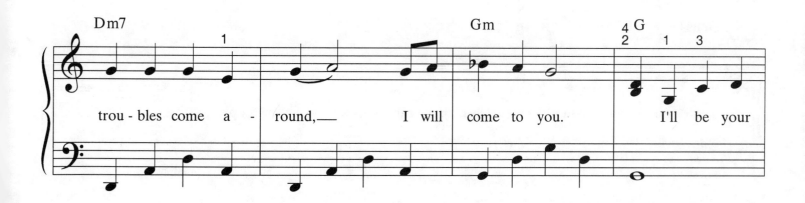

I'll Be - 5 - 2

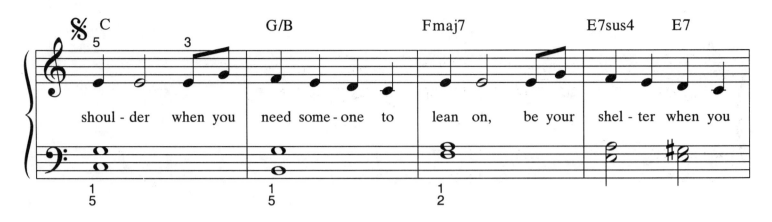

shoul - der when you | need some - one to | lean on, be your | shel - ter when you

need some - one to see you through. | I'll be there to car - ry you. | I'll be——

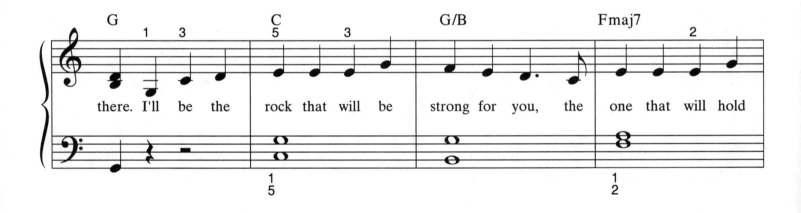

there. I'll be the | rock that will be | strong for you, the | one that will hold

on to you. When | you feel that rain—— fall - ing down,

when there's no - bod - y else_____ a - round,_____ I'll

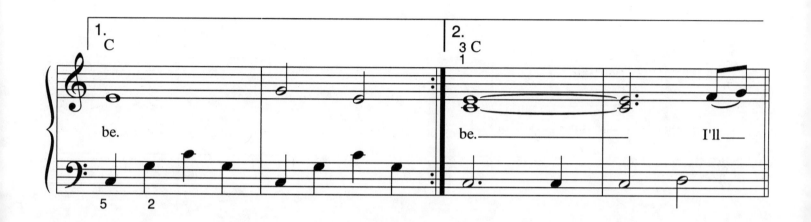

be. be._____ I'll_____

be the sun_____ when your heart's filled with rain._____ I'll_____

be the one_____ to chase the rain a - way. I'll be your

Coda

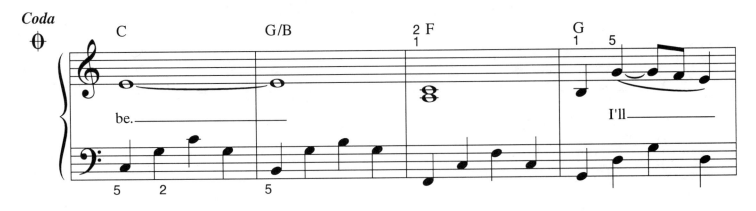

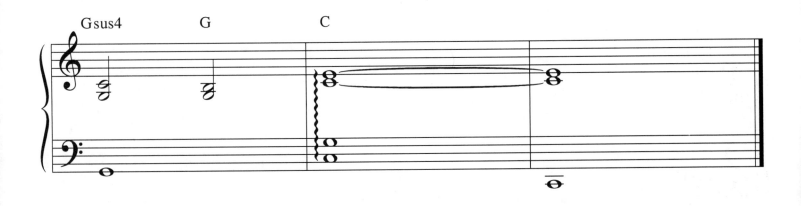

Verse 2:
And when you're there with no one there to hold,
I'll be the arms that reach for you.
And when you feel your faith is running low,
I'll be there to believe in you.
When all you find are lies,
I'll be the truth you need.
When you need someone to run to,
You can run to me.
(To Chorus:)

Your Love Amazes Me

Recorded by John Berry

Words and Music by
CHUCK JONES and AMANDA HUNT
Arranged by Richard Bradley

Your Love Amazes Me - 5 - 1

1. I've seen the sev - en won - ders of the world.

I've seen the beau - ty of dia - monds and pearls.

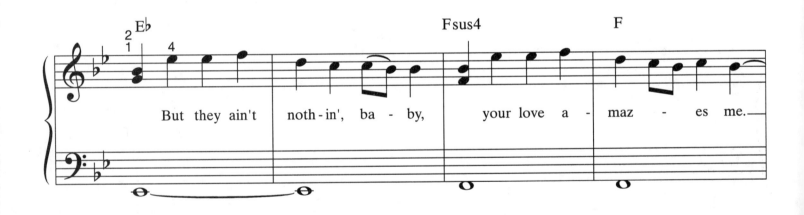

But they ain't noth - in', ba - by, your love a - maz - es me.

To next strain

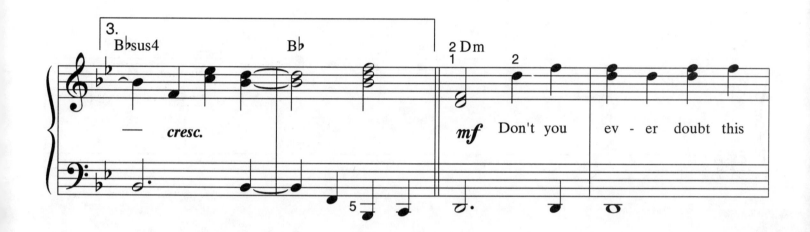

mf Don't you ev - er doubt this

love of mine. You're the on - ly one for

me. You give me hope, you give me rea - son.

28

You give me some-thing—— to be-lieve—— in. For - ev - er

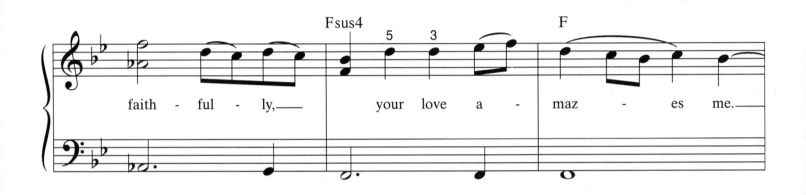

faith - ful - ly,—— your love a - maz - es me.——

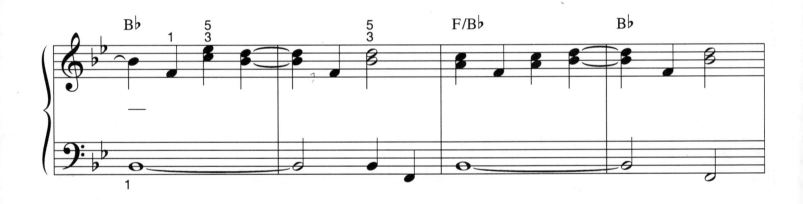

Verse 2:
I've seen a sunset that would make you cry,
And colors of a rainbow reaching 'cross the sky.
The moon in all its phases, but
Your love amazes me.
(To Chorus:)

Verse 3:
I've prayed for miracles that never came.
I got down on my knees in the pouring rain.
But only you could save me,
Your love amazes me.
(To Chorus:)

Hopelessly Devoted to You

Recorded by Olivia Newton-John

Words and Music by
JOHN FARRAR
Arranged by Richard Bradley

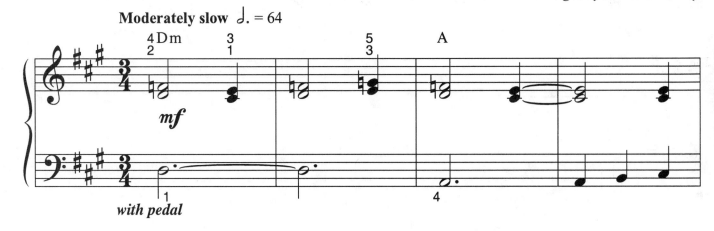

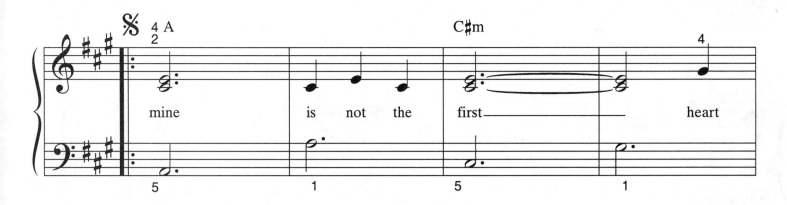

Hopelessly Devoted to You - 6 - 1

31

Verse 2:
I know I'm just a fool
Who's willin' to sit around and wait for you.
But, baby, can't you see
There's nothin' else for me to do?

Verse 3:
My head is sayin', "Fool forget him."
My heart is sayin', "Don't let go.
Hold on to the end."
And that's what I intend to do.

The Keeper of the Stars

Recorded by Tracy Byrd

Words and Music by
DICKEY LEE, DANNY MAYO
and KAREN STALEY
Arranged by Richard Bradley

The Keeper of the Stars - 4 - 1

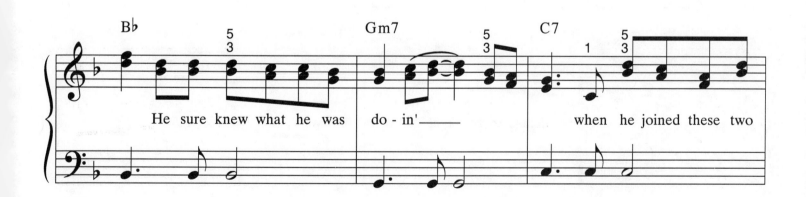

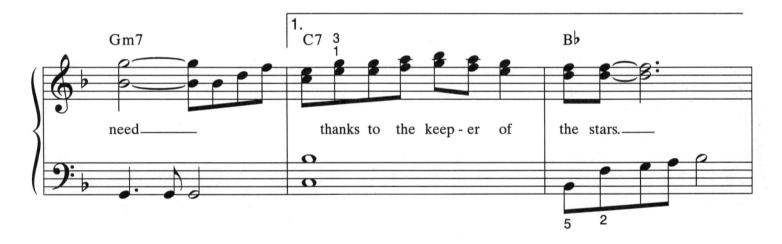

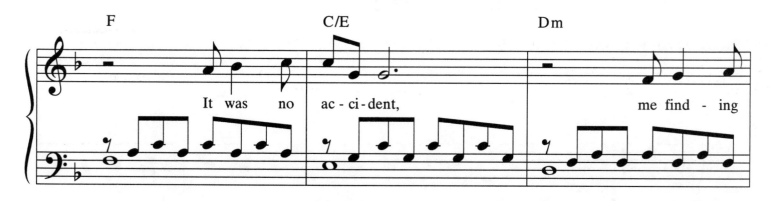

Verse 2:
Soft moonlight on your face, oh how you shine!
It takes my breath away just to look into your eyes.
I know I don't deserve a treasure like you.
There really are no words to show my gratitude.

The Keeper of the Stars - 4 - 4

You're Still the One

Recorded by Shania Twain

Words and Music by
SHANIA TWAIN and R. J. LANGE
Arranged by Richard Bradley

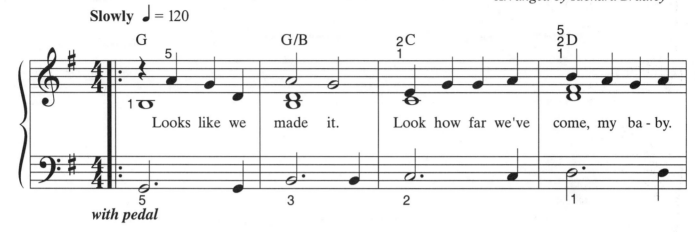

Looks like we made it. Look how far we've come, my ba - by.

with pedal

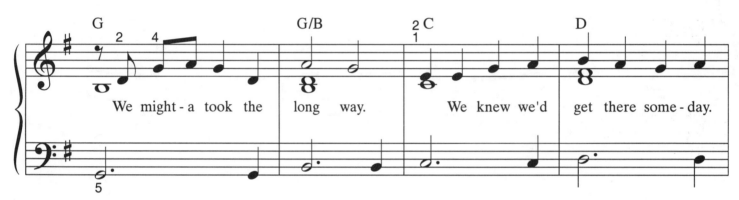

We might - a took the long way. We knew we'd get there some - day.

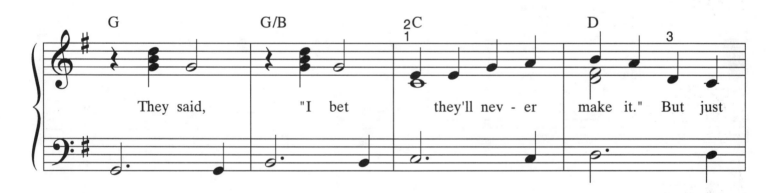

They said, "I bet they'll nev - er make it." But just

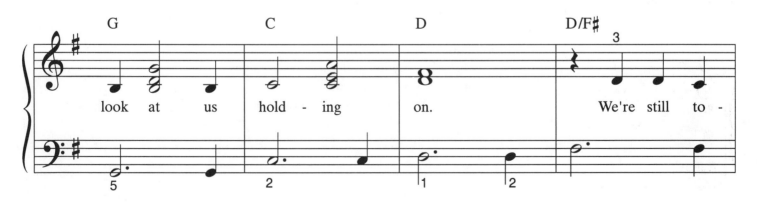

look at us hold - ing on. We're still to -

You're Still the One - 3 - 1

You're Still the One - 3 - 2

42

D.S. 𝄋 *al Coda* 𝄌

Coda 𝄌

night.

You're still the one.

night.

I'm so glad we made it.

Look how far we've come, my ba - by.

Verse 2:
Ain't nothin' better,
We beat the odds together.
I'm glad we didn't listen.
Look at what we would be missin'.

Breathe

Recorded by Faith Hill

Words and Music by
STEPHANIE BENTLEY
and HOLLY LAMAR
Arranged by Richard Bradley

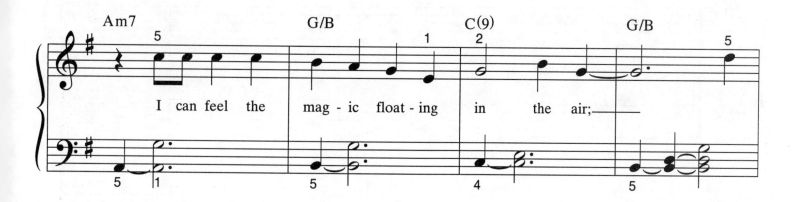

I can feel the mag - ic float - ing in the air;

be - ing— with you gets me that way.

Breathe - 5 - 1

44

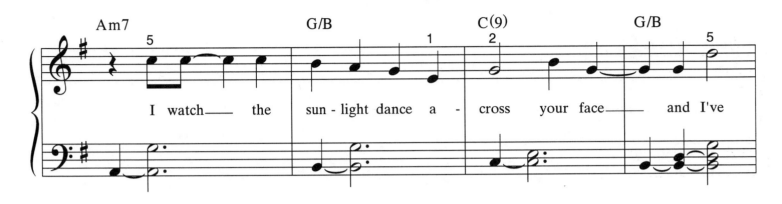

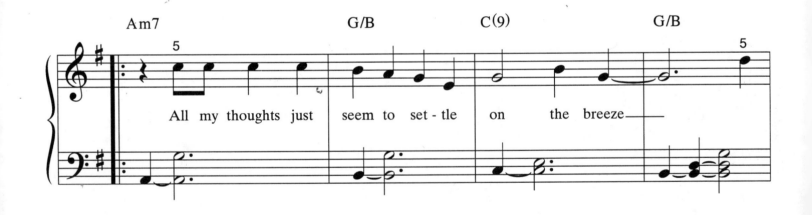

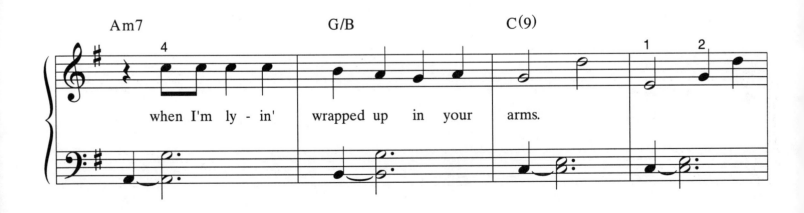

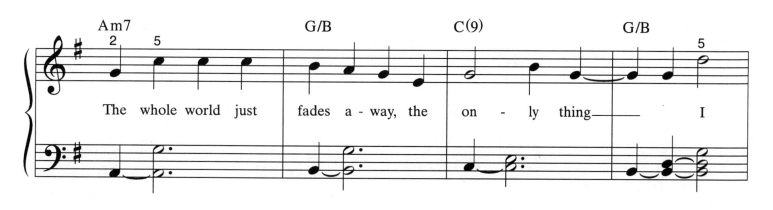

The whole world just fades a-way, the on - ly thing____ I

hear is the beat-ing of your heart.____ 'Cause I can feel you

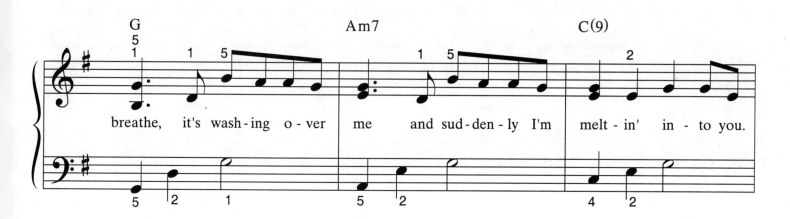

breathe, it's wash-ing o-ver me and sud-den-ly I'm melt-in' in-to you.

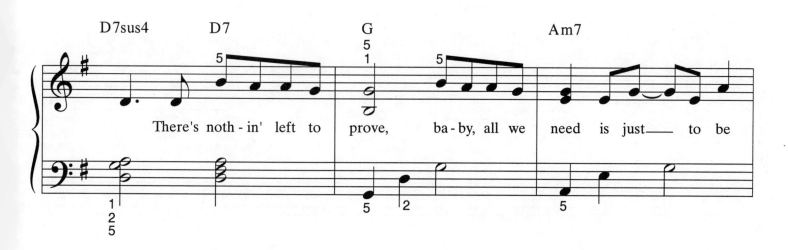

There's noth-in' left to prove, ba-by, all we need is just____ to be

Breathe - 5 - 3

Verse 2:
In a way, I know my heart is waking up
As all the walls come tumblin' down.
Closer than I've ever felt before
And I know and you know
There's no need for words right now.

Some Things Never Change

Recorded by Tim McGraw

Words and Music by
BRAD CRISLER and WALT ALDRIDGE
Arranged by Richard Bradley

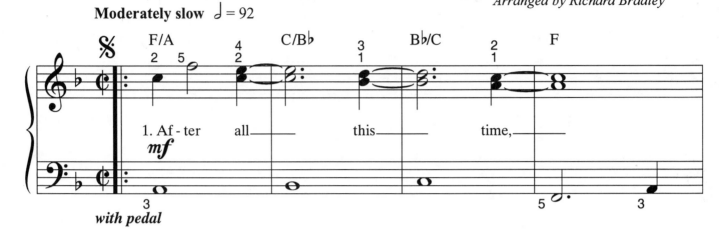

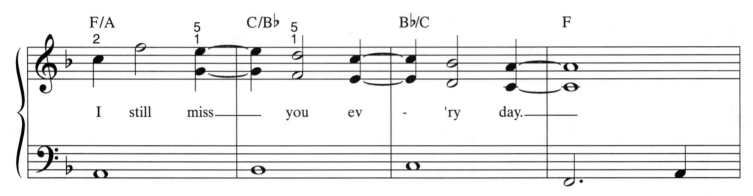

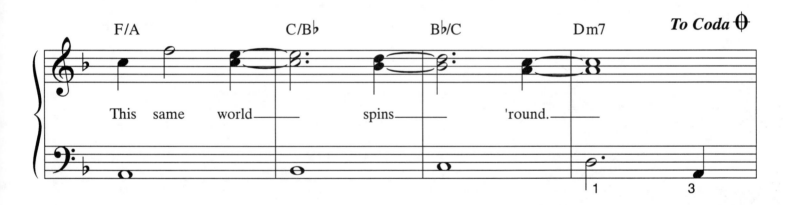

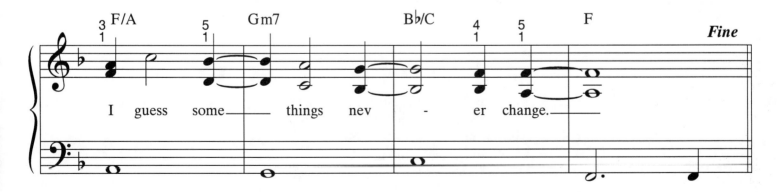

Some Things Never Change - 4 - 1

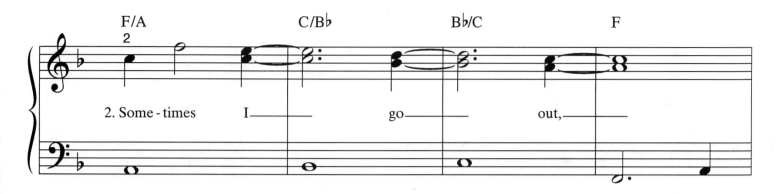

2. Some - times I_____ go____ out,____

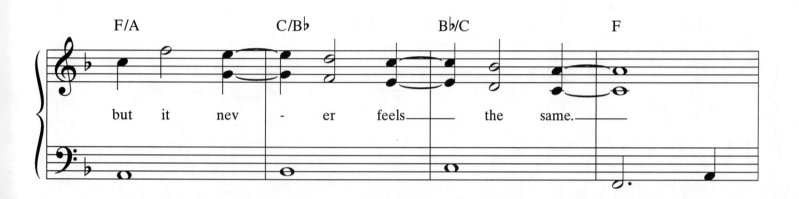

but it nev - er feels____ the same.____

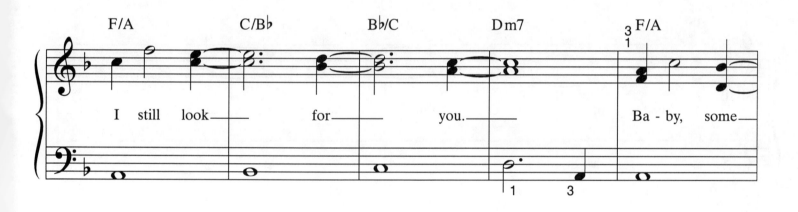

I still look____ for____ you.____ Ba - by, some____

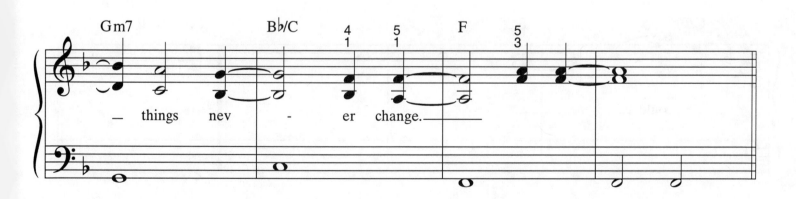

____ things nev - er change.____

When I said ___ I'd love ___ you for ___ e - ter -

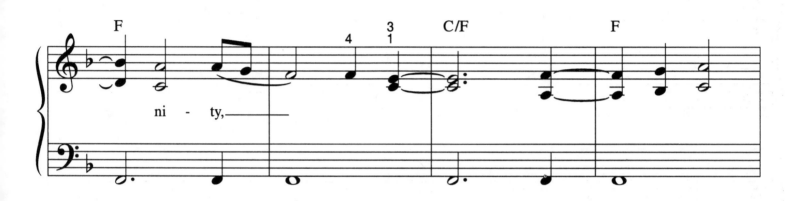

ni - ty, ___

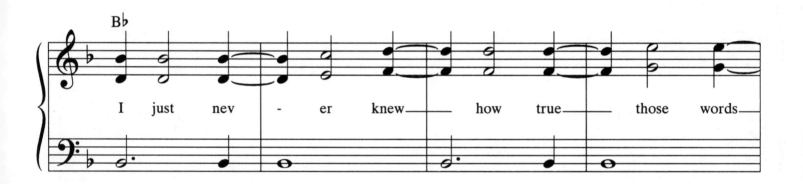

I just nev - er knew ___ how true ___ those words ___

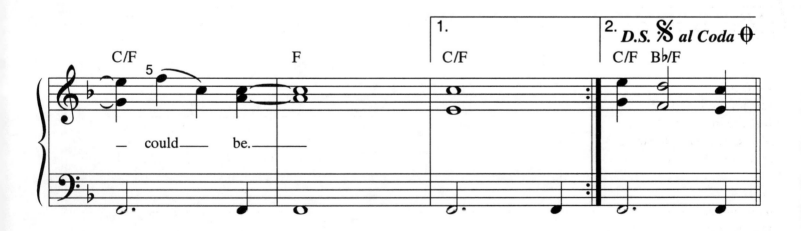

___ could ___ be. ___

Coda

Verse 3:
Just an old love song,
Just the mention of your name,
My heart breaks in two again.
I guess some things never change.

Verse 4:
Instrumental
Maybe someday someone else
Will set me free.
Until then, I'll live with your love's legacy.

Verse 5:
I'll keep holding on,
Hoping you'll come back someday.
You can rest assured,
Baby, some things never change.
Girl, I'm still in love with you.
I guess somethings never change.

The Little Girl

Recorded by John Michael Montgomery

Words and Music by
HARLEY ALLEN
Arranged by Richard Bradley

The Little Girl - 4 - 1

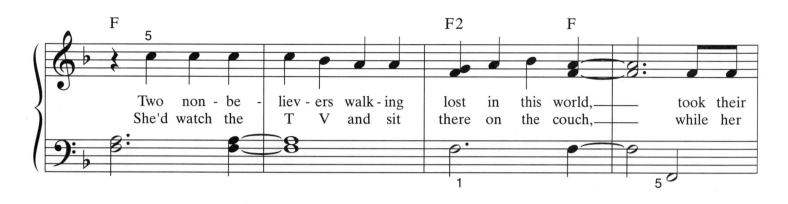

Two non-be- liev-ers walk-ing lost in this world,___ took their
She'd watch the T V and sit there on the couch,___ while her

1.

ba-by with them.___ What a sad lit-tle girl.___
mom fell a-sleep___ and her

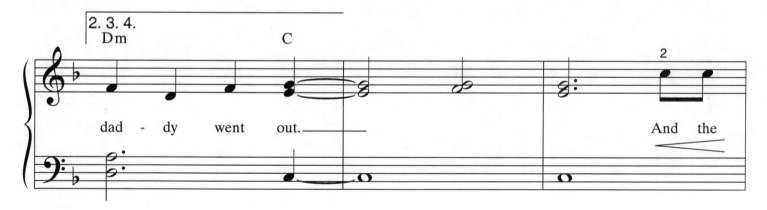

2. 3. 4.

dad-dy went out.___ And the

Chorus:

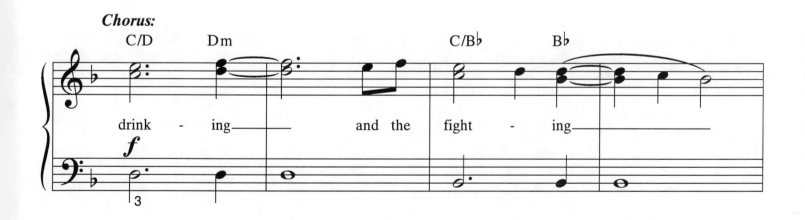

drink - ing___ and the fight - ing___

f

54

just got worse___ ev - 'ry night.___ Be - hind

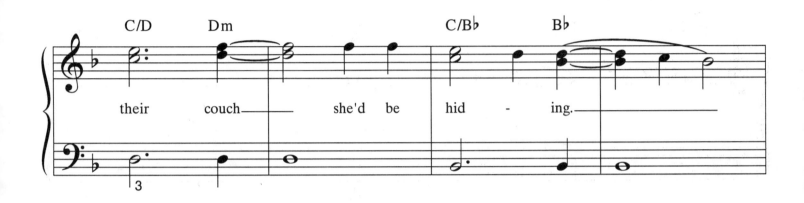

their couch___ she'd be hid - ing.___

Oh, what a sad lit - tle life.___

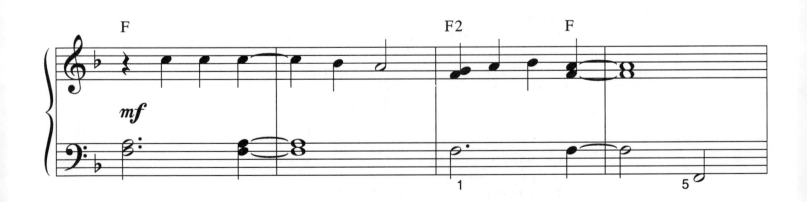

The Little Girl - 4 - 3

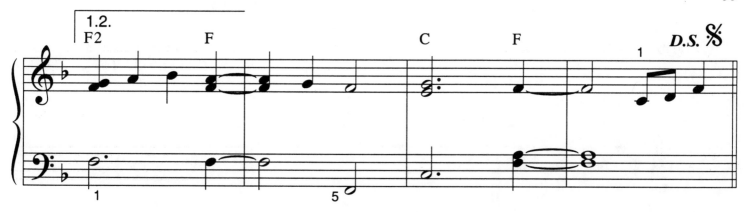

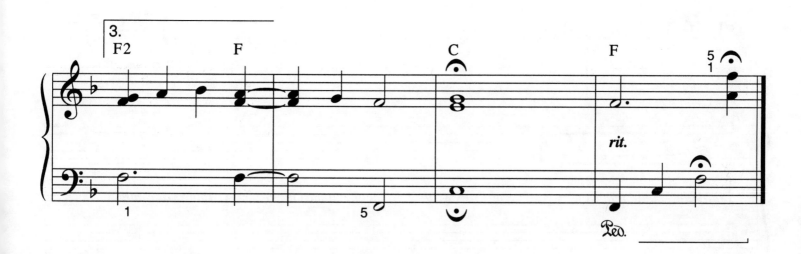

Verse 3:
And like it always does, the bad just got worse,
With every slap and every curse,
Until her daddy, in a drunk rage one night,
Used a gun on her mom and then took his life.

Chorus 2:
And some people from the city
Took the girl far away
To a new mom and a new dad,
Kisses and hugs every day.

Verse 4:
Her first day of Sunday school, the teacher walked in,
And a small little girl stared at a picture of Him.
She said, "I know that man up there on that cross.
I don't know his name, but I know he got off."

Chorus 3:
"Cause He was there in my old house
And held me close to His side
As I hid there behind our couch
The night that my parents died."

Couldn't Last a Moment

Recorded by Collin Raye

Words and Music by
DANNY WELLS and JEFFREY STEELE
Arranged by Richard Bradley

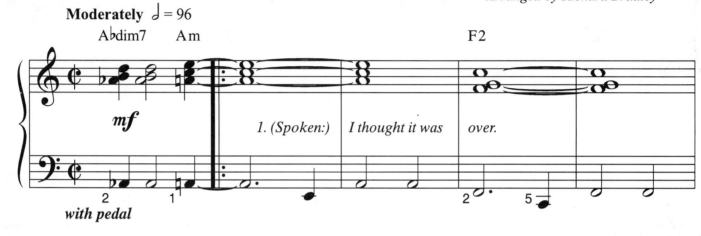

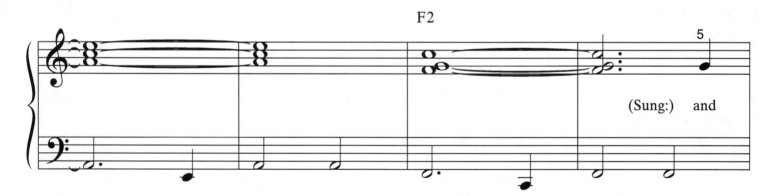

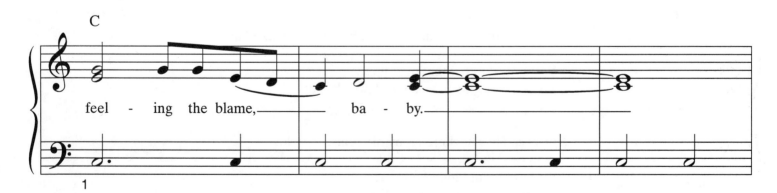

Couldn't Last a Moment - 5 - 1

Thought I could quit you, but I still miss your love.

What was I think - ing, think - ing I could still walk down the

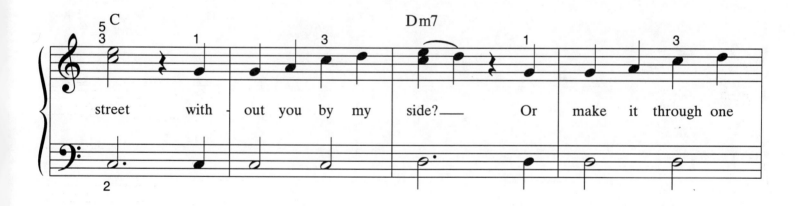

street with - out you by my side?___ Or make it through one

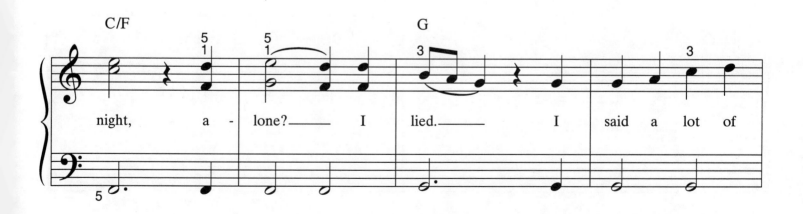

night, a - lone?___ I lied.___ I said a lot of

Couldn't Last a Moment - 5 - 2

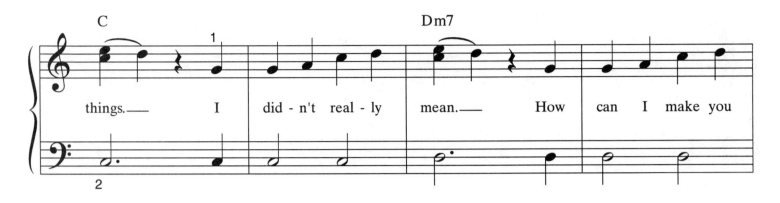

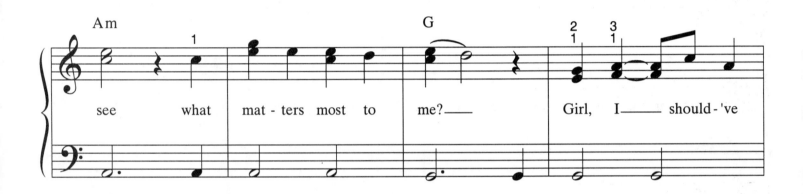

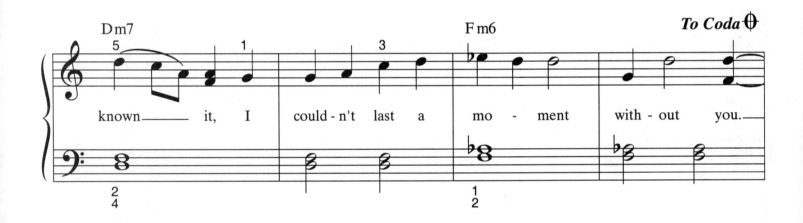

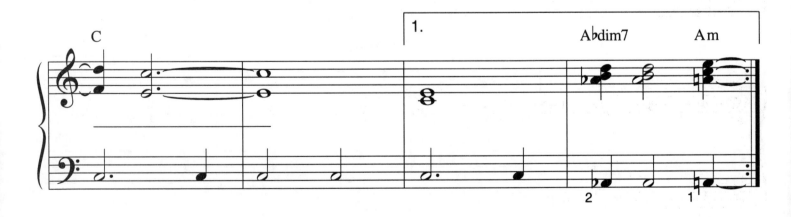

Coda

Oh,_____ girl,____ I should-'ve____ known____

it, I could-n't last a mo - ment____

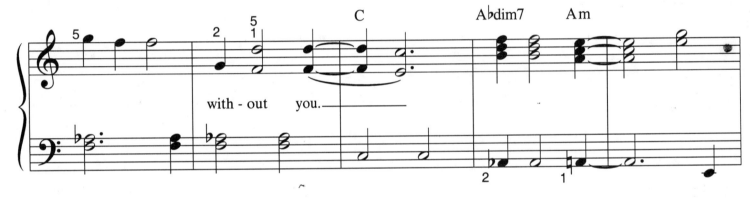

with - out you.____

Verse 2:
(Spoken:)
You've got every right
To turn and walk away.
I can't make you stay.
I broke your heart,
That's the bottom line.
(Sung:)
I wasted so much precious time.
I see you with your friends
Wearing a smile again.
What was I thinking,
Thinking I could still walk down the street...

How Do I Live

From the Motion Picture *Con Air*
Recorded by by Trisha Yearwood

Words and Music by
DIANE WARREN
Arranged by Richard Bradley

How Do I Live - 5 - 1

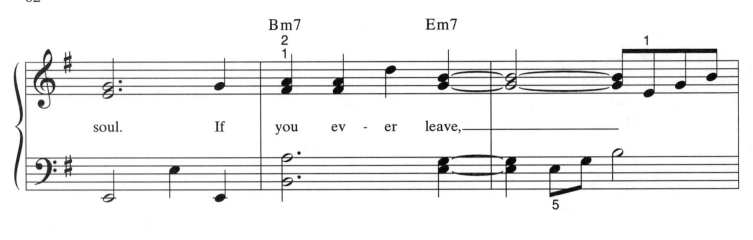

soul.   If   you   ev - er   leave,_____

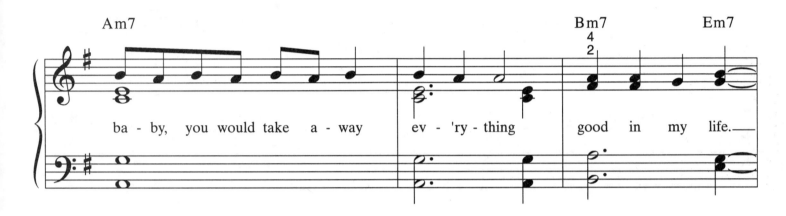

ba - by,   you would take   a - way   ev - 'ry-thing   good   in   my   life._____

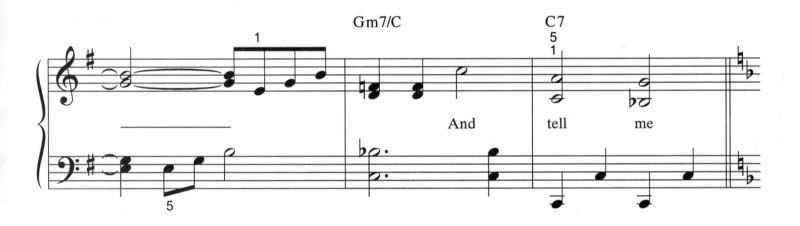

And   tell   me

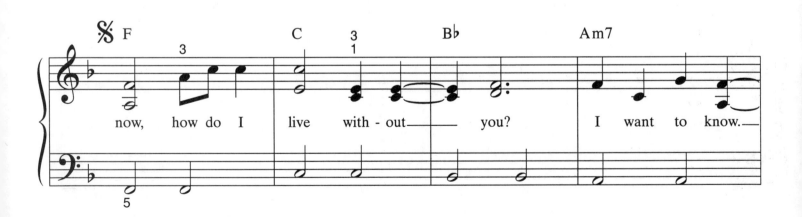

now,   how do I   live   with - out_____   you?   I   want   to   know._____

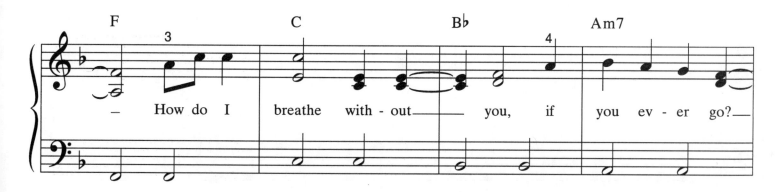

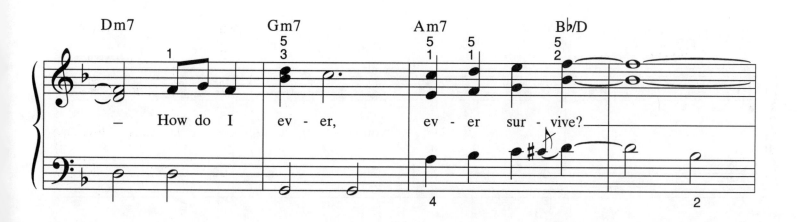

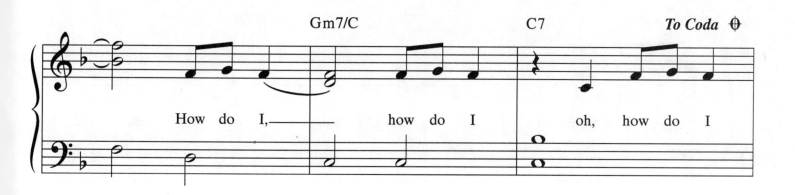

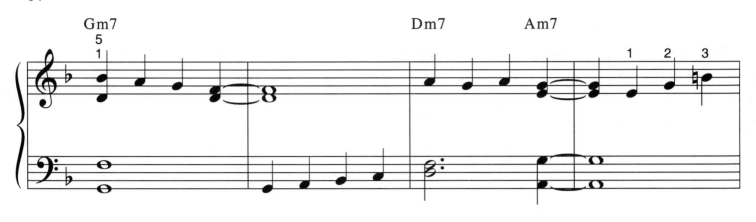

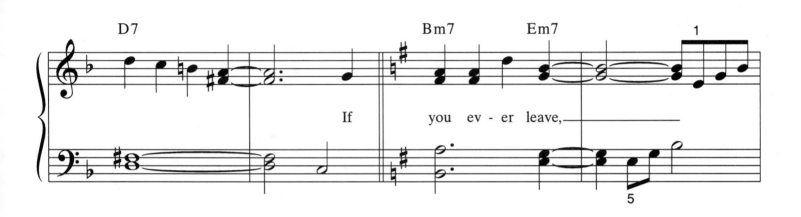

If you ev - er leave,

ba - by, you would take a - way ev - 'ry - thing. Need you with me.

Ba - by, 'cause you know that you're ev - 'ry - thing

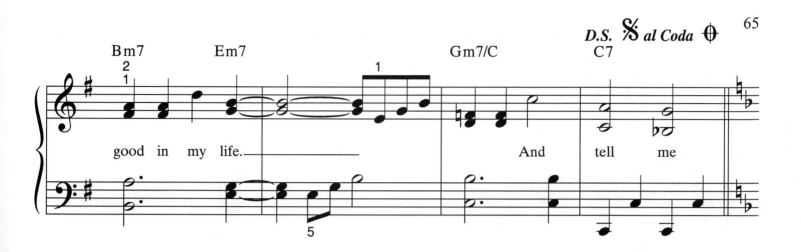

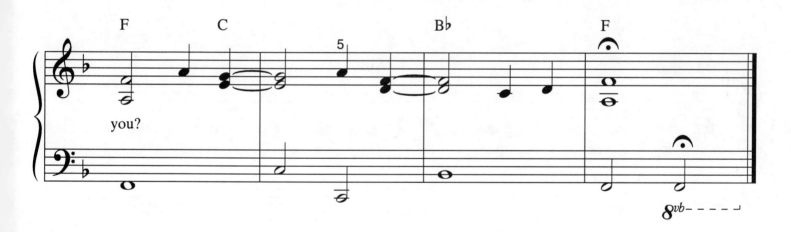

Verse 2:
Without you, there'd be no sun in my sky,
There would be no love in my life,
There'd be no world left for me
And I, baby, I don't know what I woould do,
I'd be lost if I lost you.
If you ever leave,
Baby, you would take away everything real in my life,
And tell me now. . .
(To Chorus:).

You Light Up My Life

Recorded by LeAnn Rimes

Words and Music by
JOE BROOKS
Arranged by Richard Bradley

So man-y nights____ I'd sit by my win-dow,

wait - ing for some - one to sing me his song.

So man - y dreams____ I kept deep in - side me, a -

You Light Up My Life - 4 - 1

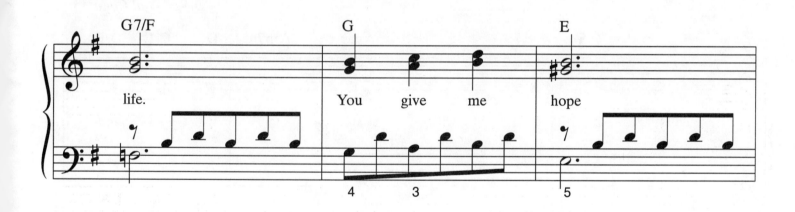

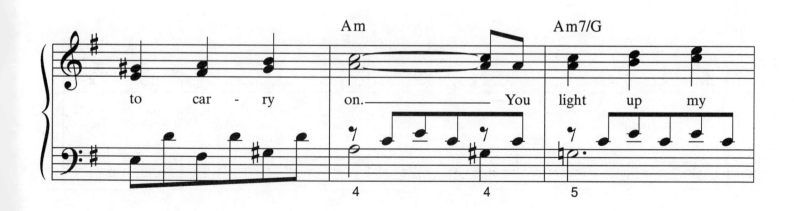

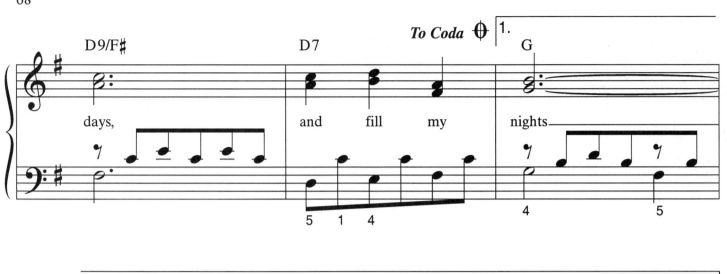

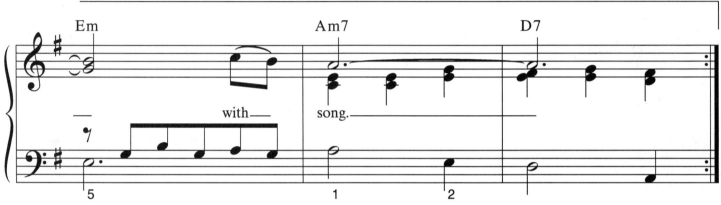

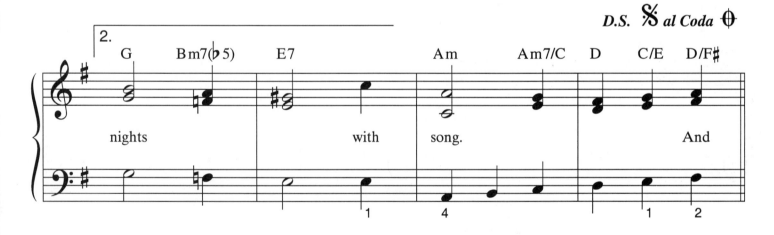

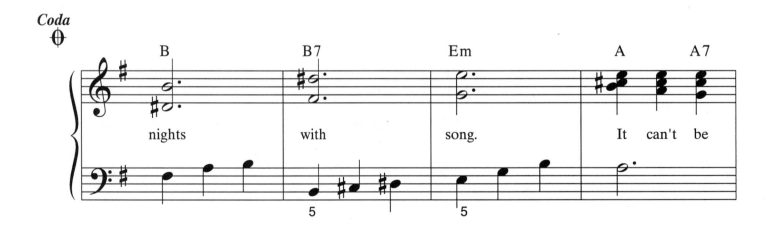

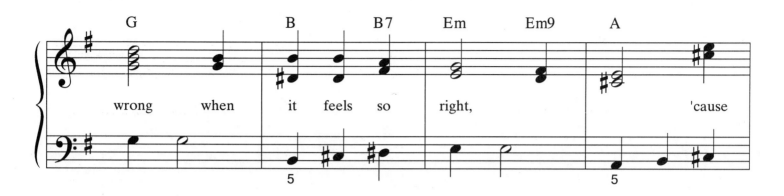

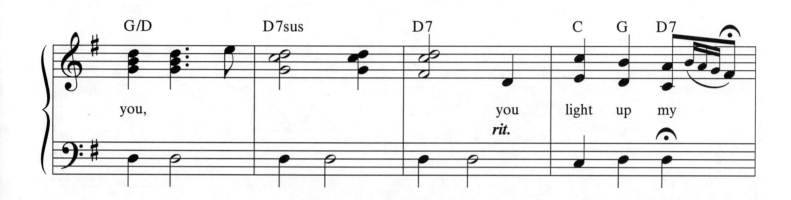

Verse 2:
Rollin' at sea, adrift on the waters,
Could it be finally I'm turning for home?
Finally a chance to say, "Hey! I love you."
Never again to be all alone.
Chorus:

WWW.Memory

Recorded by Alan Jackson

Words and Music by
ALAN JACKSON
Arranged by Richard Bradley

I know you're leav - ing, I see the signs.___ You're gon - na walk out___ on this heart of

WWW.Memory - 6 - 1

72

WWW.Memory - 6 - 3

74

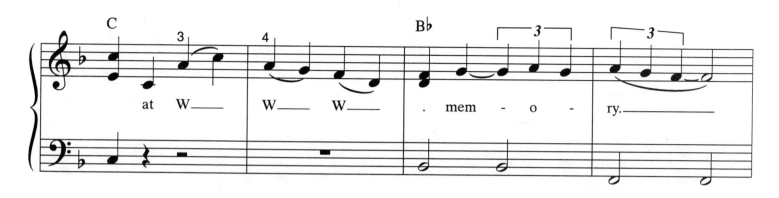

at W———— W———— W———— .mem - o - ry.————

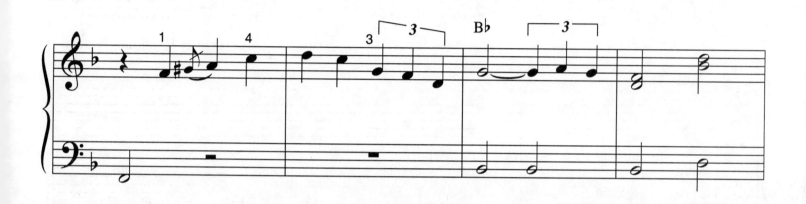

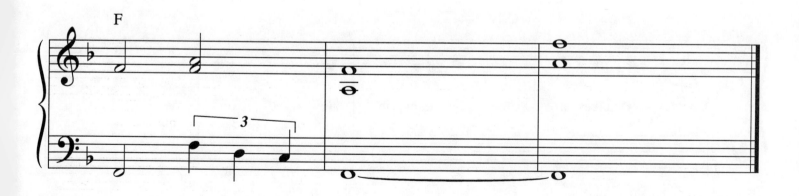

Behind Closed Doors

Recorded by Charlie Rich

Words and Music by
KENNY O'DELL
Arranged by Richard Bradley

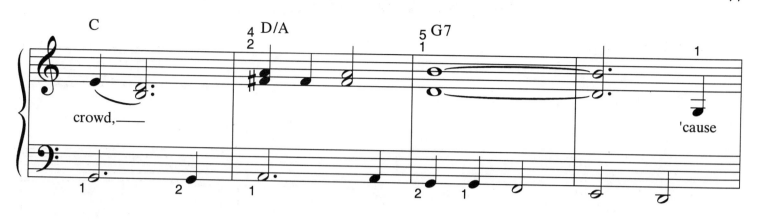

crowd,_____ 'cause

peo - ple like to talk,_____ Lord, don't they love_____ to_____

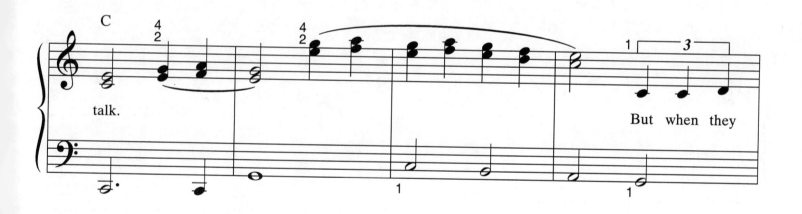

talk. But when they

turn out the_____ lights, I know she'll be leav - in'_____ with

78

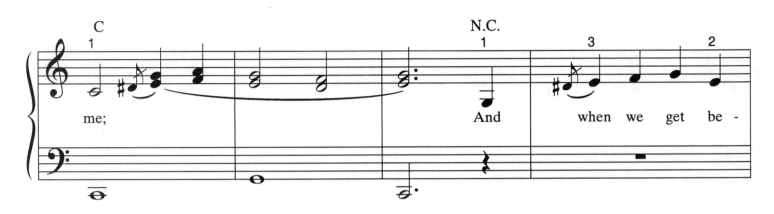

me;   And   when we get be -

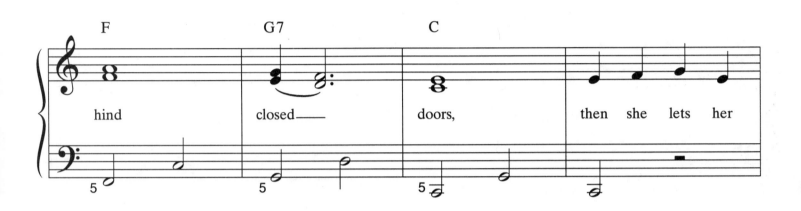

hind   closed   doors,   then she lets her

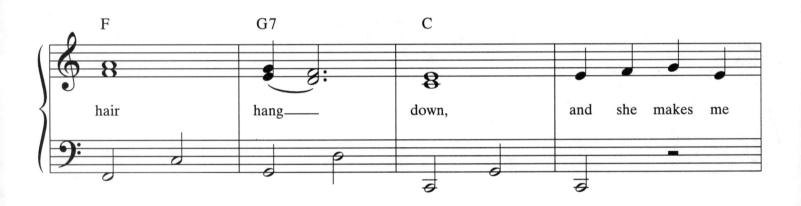

hair   hang   down,   and she makes me

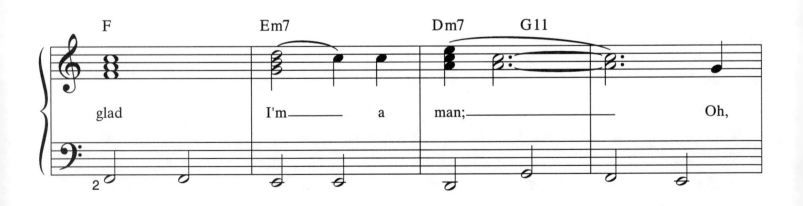

glad   I'm   a   man;   Oh,

Behind Closed Doors - 4 - 3

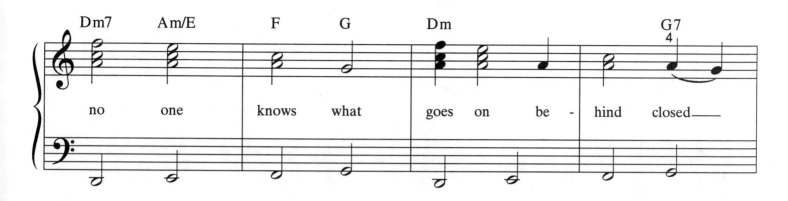

no one knows what goes on be - hind closed

doors. My

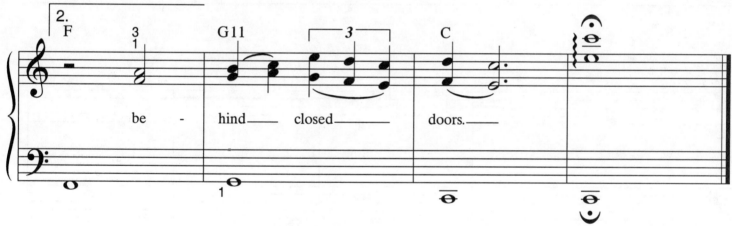

be - hind closed doors.

Verse 2:
My baby makes me smile,
Lord, don't she make me smile.
She's never far away
Or too tired to say, "I want you."
She's always a lady,
Just like a lady should be.
But when they turn out the lights,
She's still a baby to me.

Rhinestone Cowboy

Recorded by Glen Campbell

Words and Music by
LARRY WEISS
Arranged by Richard Bradley

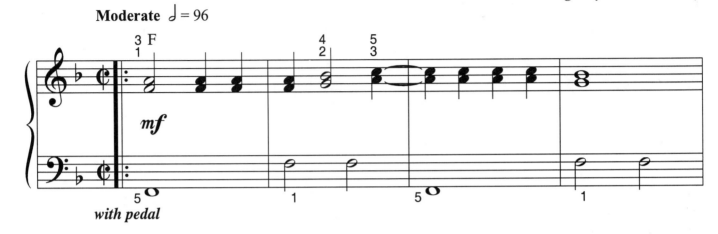

I've been

walk - in' these streets so long,

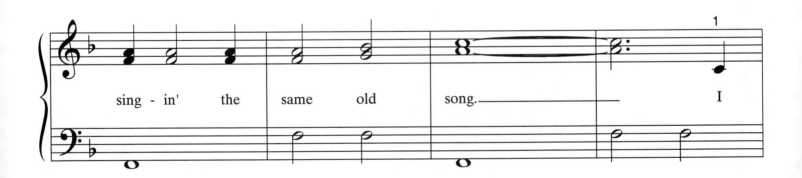

sing - in' the same old song. I

Rhinestone Cowboy - 5 - 1

know ev - 'ry crack on these dir - ty side - walks of

Broad - way; where

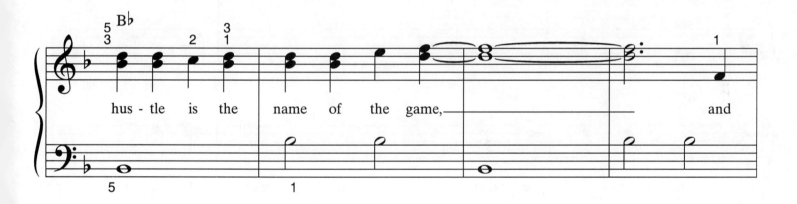

hus - tle is the name of the game, and

nice guys get washed a - way like the snow and the

84

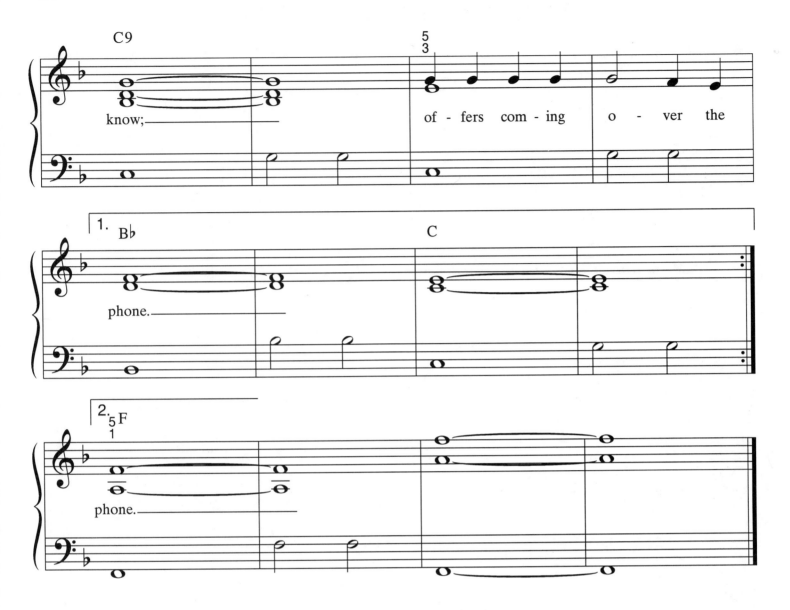

Verse 2:
Well, I really don't mind the rain
And a smile can hide the pain;
But you're down when you're riding a train
That's taking the long way.
But I dream of the things I'll do
With a subway token and a dollar
Tucked inside my shoe.
There's been a load of compromisin'
On the road to my horizon;
But I'm gonna be where the lights are shinin' on me.
To Chorus:
Like a rhinestone cowboy...

Man! I Feel Like a Woman!

Recorded by Shania Twain

Words and Music by
SHANIA TWAIN and R.J. LANGE
Arranged by Richard Bradley

Moderate shuffle rock ♩ = 120

Let's go, girls. I'm go-ing out to-night. I'm

feel-in' al-right. Gon-na let it all hang out.____

Wan-na make some noise, real-ly raise my voice. Yeah, I wan-na scream and

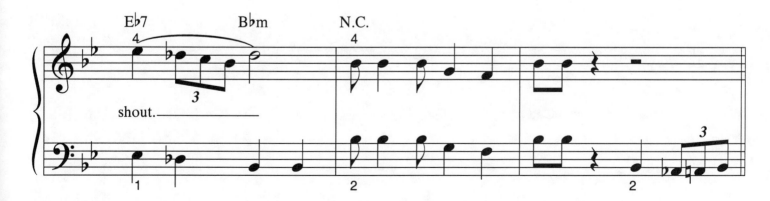

shout.____

Man! I Feel Like a Woman! - 5 - 1

No in-hi-bi-tions, make no con-di-tions. Get a lit-tle out of

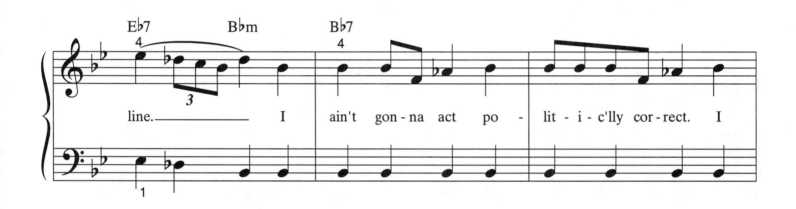

line._____ I ain't gon-na act po - lit-i-c'lly cor-rect. I

on-ly wan-na have a good time._____ The best thing a-bout___

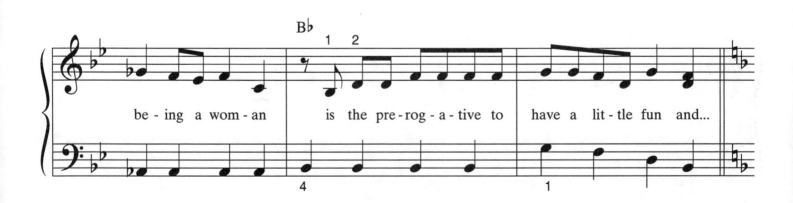

be-ing a wom-an is the pre-rog-a-tive to have a lit-tle fun and...

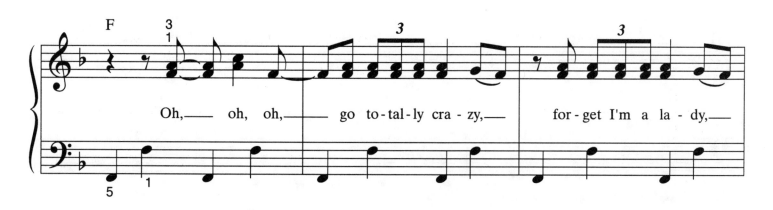

Oh,— oh, oh,— go to-tal-ly cra-zy,— for-get I'm a la-dy,—

men's shirts, short skirts, oh,— oh, oh,— real-ly go wild, yeah,—

do-in' it in style.— Oh,— oh, oh,— get in the ac-tion,—

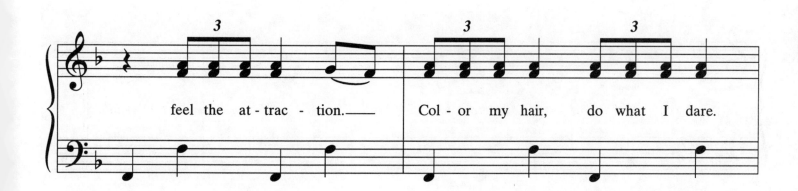

feel the at-trac-tion.— Col-or my hair, do what I dare.

Oh,—— oh, oh,—— I wan-na be free, yeah, to feel the way I

feel.———— *Man!* I feel—— like a wom - an.

The

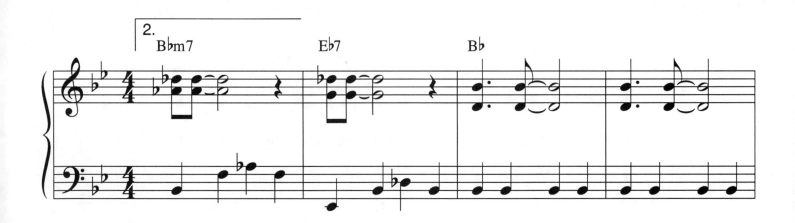

Verse 2:
The girls need a break.
Tonight we're gonna take
The chance to get out on the town.
We don't need romance.
We only wanna dance.
We're gonna let our hair hang down.
The best thing about being a woman
Is the prerogative to have a little fun and...
(To Chorus:)

My Maria

Recorded by Brooks & Dunn

Words and Music by
DANIEL J. MOORE and B.W. STEVENSON
Arranged by Richard Bradley

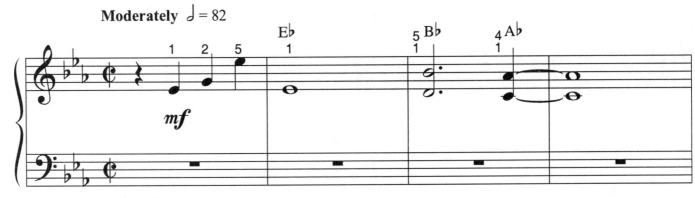

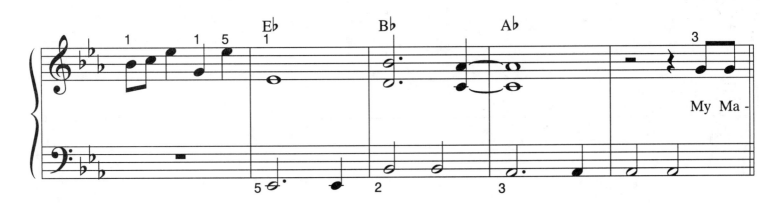

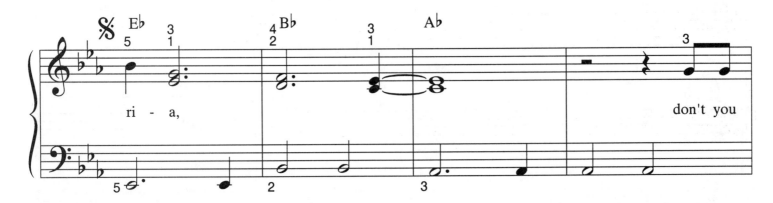

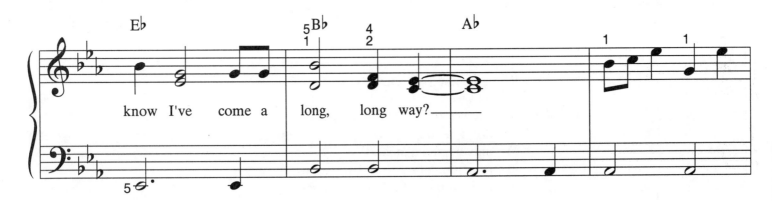

My Maria - 6 - 1

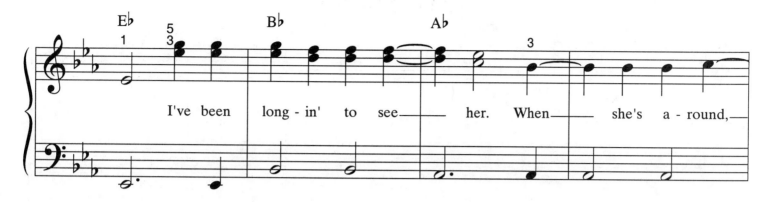

I've been   long - in' to see___ her. When___ she's   a - round,___

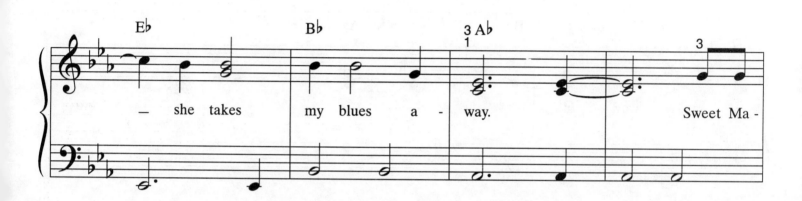

___ she takes   my blues a - way.   Sweet Ma -

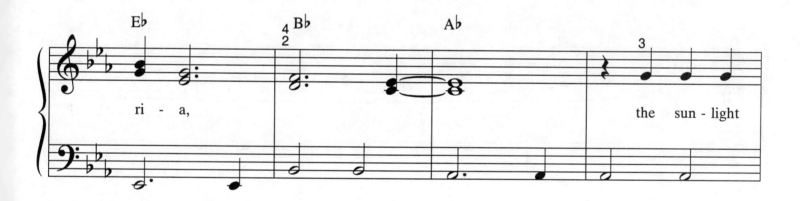

ri - a,   the sun - light

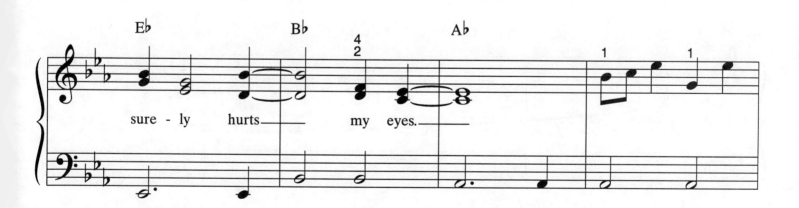

sure - ly hurts___ my eyes.___

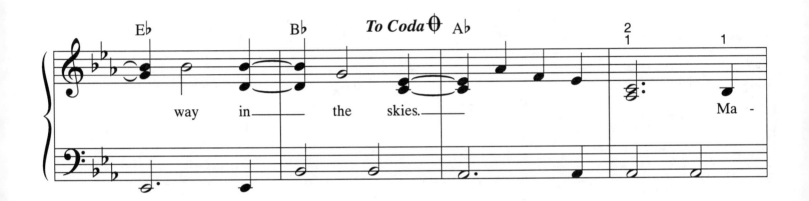

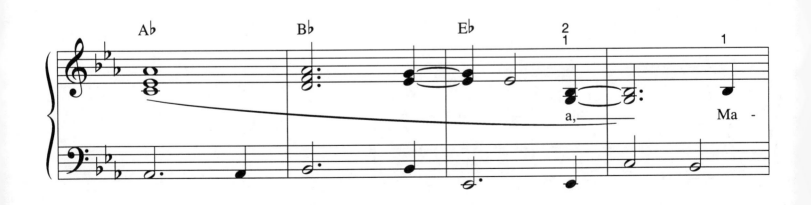

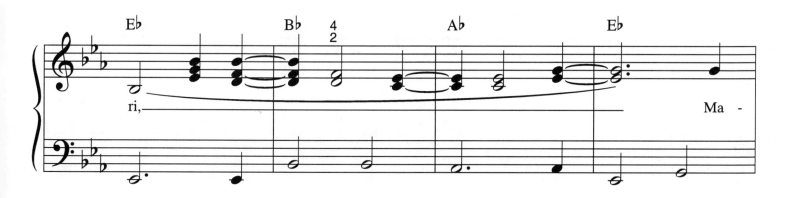

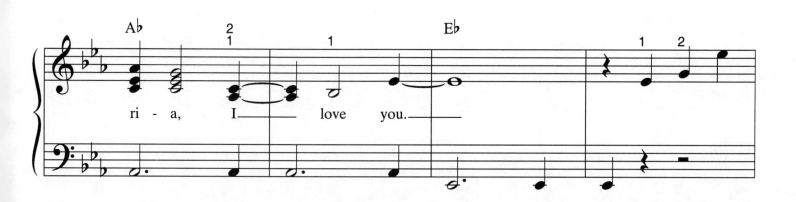

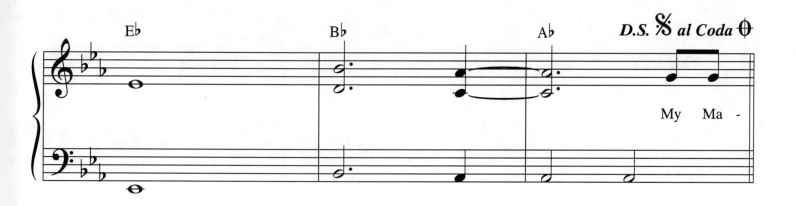

Coda

94

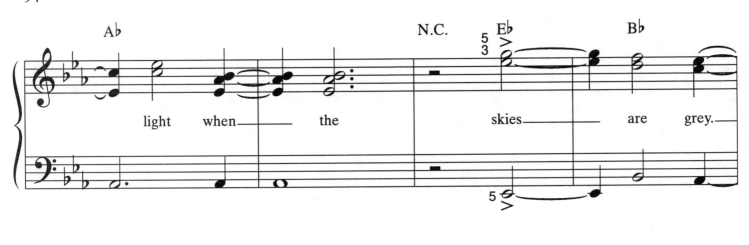

light when the skies are grey.

She treats me so

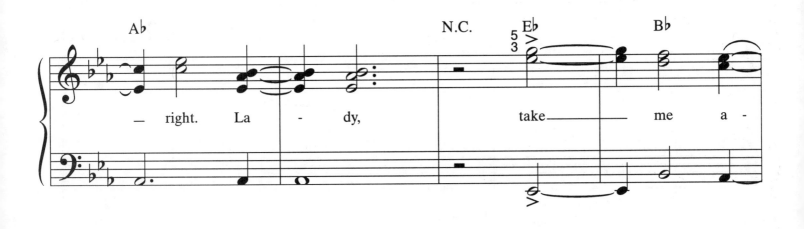

right. La - dy, take me a -

way.

My Maria - 6 - 5

Verse 2:

My Maria, there were some blue and sorrowed times.
Just my thoughts about you bring back my peace of mind.
Gypsy lady, you're a miracle work for me.
You set my soul free like a ship sailin' on the sea.

Don't It Make My Brown Eyes Blue

Recorded by Crystal Gayle

Words and Music by
RICHARD LEIGH
Arranged by Richard Bradley

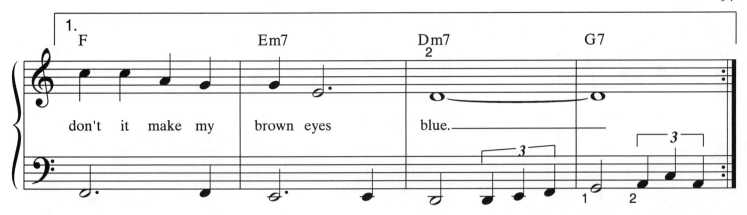

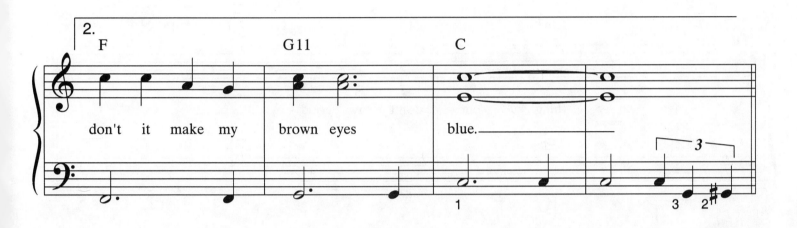

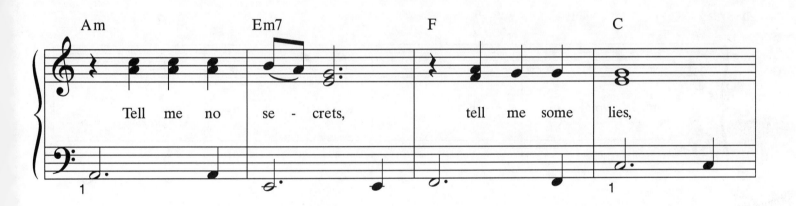

98

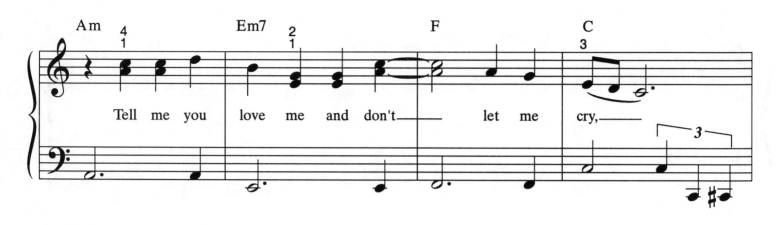

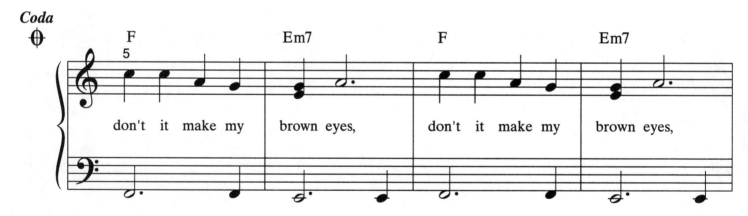

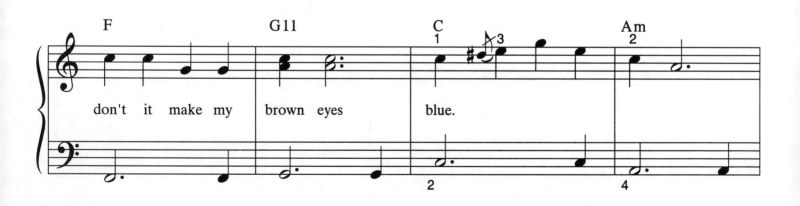

Don't It Make My Brown Eyes Blue - 4 - 3

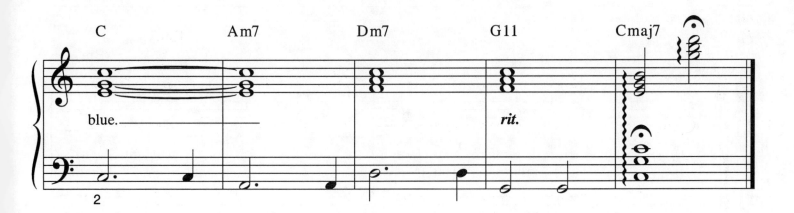

Verse 2:
I'll be fine when you're gone,
I'll just cry all night long,
Say it isn't true
And don't it make my brown eyes blue.

Verse 3:
I didn't mean to treat you bad,
Didn't know just what I had,
But honey now I do
And don't it make my brown eyes blue.

Years From Here

Recorded by Baker & Myers

Words and Music by
GARY BAKER, JERRY WILLIAMS
and FRANK J. MYERS
Arranged by Richard Bradley

Years From Here - 4 - 1

The mo-ment you took my hand_____ there was no doubt_____
I'll go a - bove and be - yond_____ to give you ev -

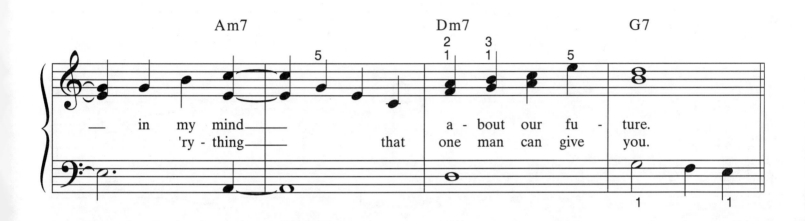

___ in my mind_____ a - bout our fu - ture.
'ry - thing_____ that one man can give you.

I don't_____ need_____ a crys - tal ball,_____
I know_____ we've just be - gun_____

through your eyes_____ I see it all._____
and the best_____ is still yet to come._____

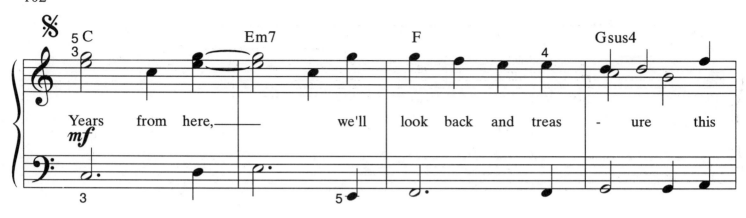

Years from here,⸺ we'll look back and treas - ure this

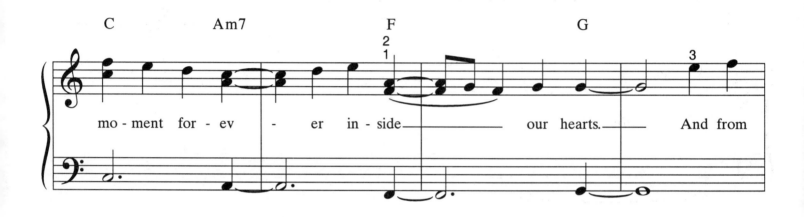

mo - ment for - ev - er in - side⸺ our hearts.⸺ And from

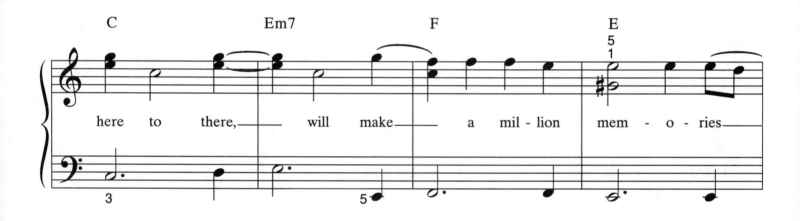

here to there,⸺ will make⸺ a mil - lion mem - o - ries⸺

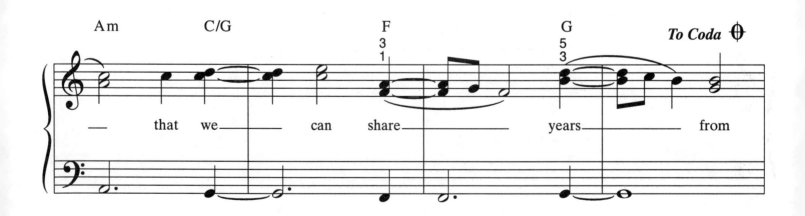

⸺ that we⸺ can share⸺ years⸺ from

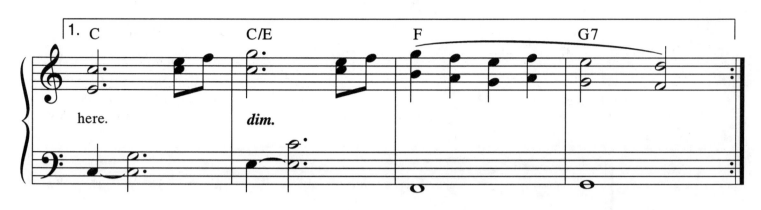

This Kiss

Recorded by Faith Hill

Words and Music by
ROBIN LERNER, ANNIE ROBOFF
and BETH NIELSEN CHAPMAN
Arranged by Richard Bradley

Moderately, with doublt-time feel ♩ = 64

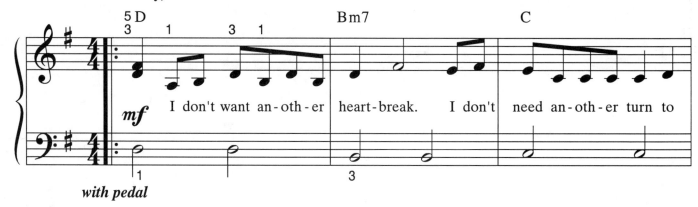

I don't want an-oth-er heart-break. I don't need an-oth-er turn to

cry,_____ no. I don't want to learn the hard way. Ba-by,

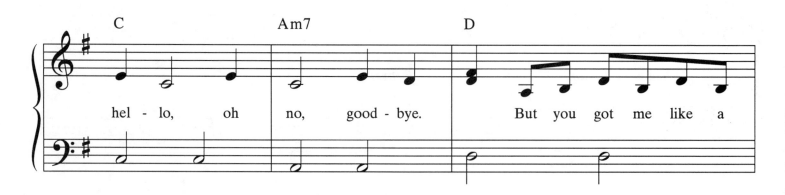

hel - lo, oh no, good - bye. But you got me like a

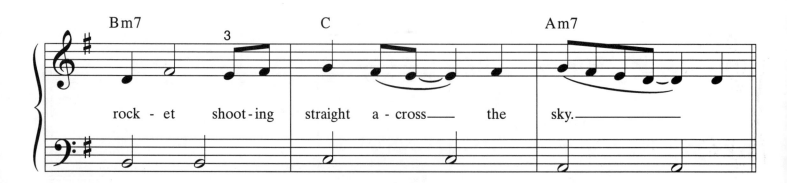

rock - et shoot-ing straight a-cross_____ the sky._____

Verse 2:
Cinderella said to Snow White,
"How does love get so off course?"
Oh. All I wanted was a white knight
With a good heart, soft touch, fast horse.
Ride me off into the sunset, baby,
I'm forever yours.

My Heroes Have Always Been Cowboys

Recorded by Willie Nelson

Words and Music by
SHARON VAUGHN
Arranged by Richard Bradley

Moderately slow ♩ = 96

with pedal

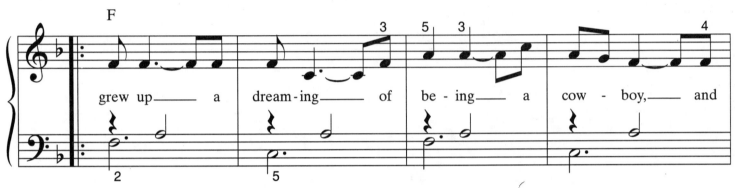

grew up___ a dream-ing___ of be-ing___ a cow - boy,___ and

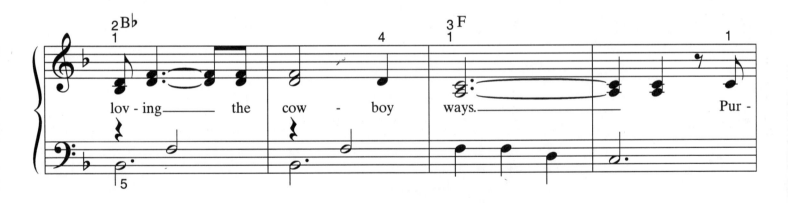

lov-ing___ the cow - boy ways.___ Pur -

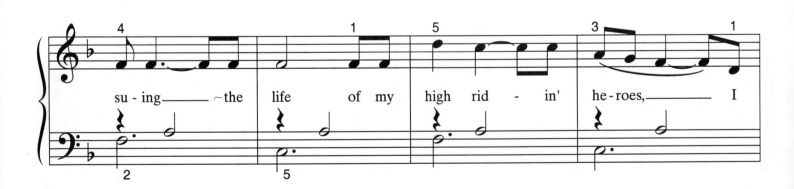

su - ing___ ~the life of my high rid - in' he-roes,___ I

My Heroes Have Always Been Cowboys - 4 - 1

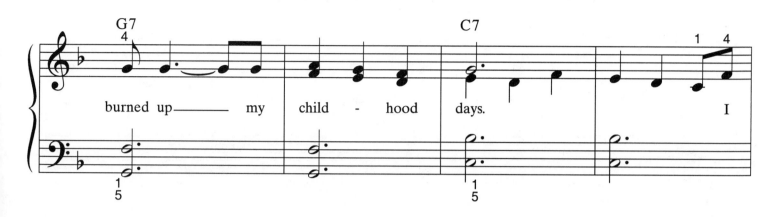

burned up———— my child - hood days.

I

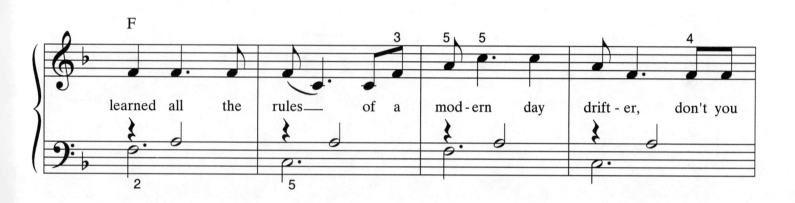

learned all the rules——— of a mod-ern day drift - er, don't you

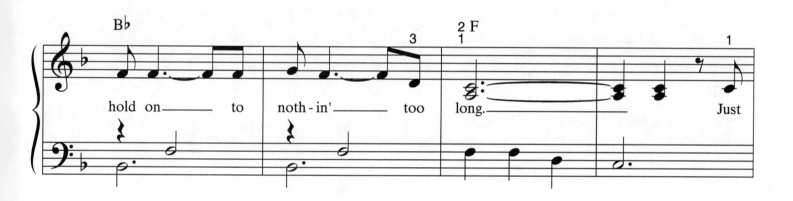

hold on——— to noth-in'——— too long.———— Just

take what——— you need—— from the la - dies then leave them with the

My Heroes Have Always Been Cowboys - 4 - 2

110

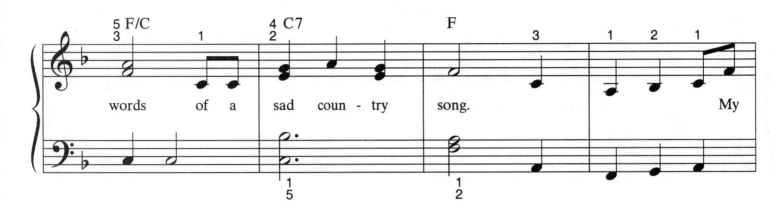

words of a sad coun-try song. My

he-roes—— have al - ways been cow-boys,——

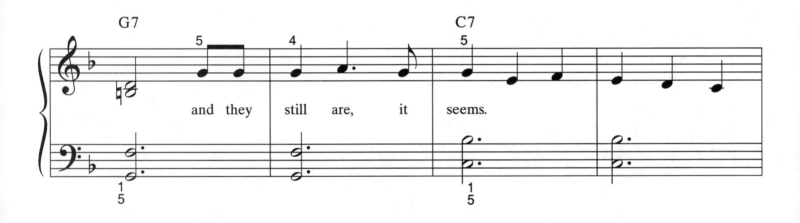

and they still are, it seems.

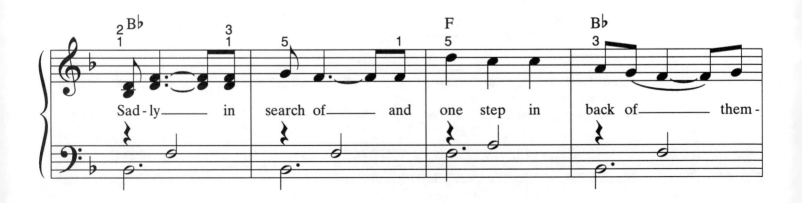

Sad-ly—— in search of—— and one step in back of—— them-

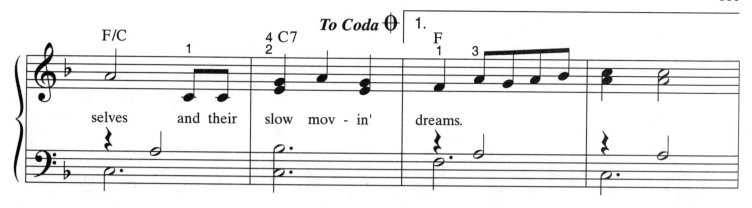

selves   and their   slow mov - in'   dreams.

dreams.   My

Coda

dreams.

Verse 2:
Cowboys are special
With their own brand of mis'ry
From being alone too long.
You could die from the cold
In the arms of a nightmare,
Knowing well that your best days are gone.
Pickin' up hookers instead of a pen
I let the words of my youth fade away.
Old worn out saddles
And old worn out mem'ries
With no one and no place to stay.

My Heroes Have Always Been Cowboys - 4 - 4

Any Day Now

Recorded by Ronnie Milsap

Words by BOB HILLIARD
Music by BURT BACHARACH
Arranged by Richard Bradley

Any Day Now - 5 - 1

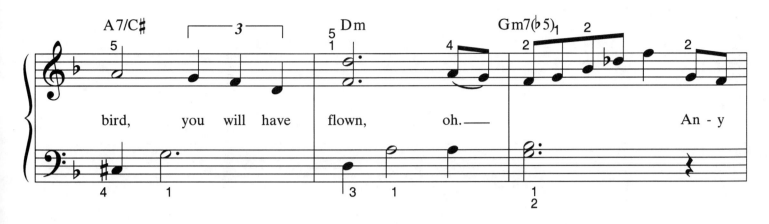

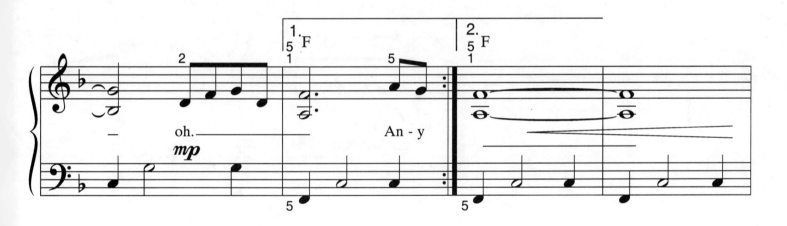

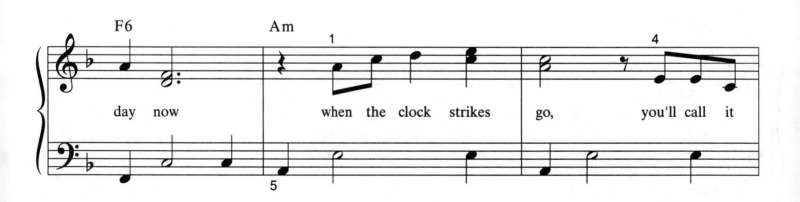

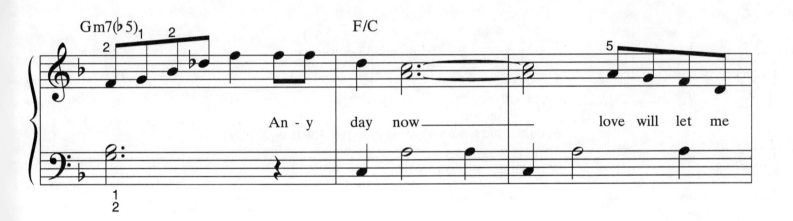

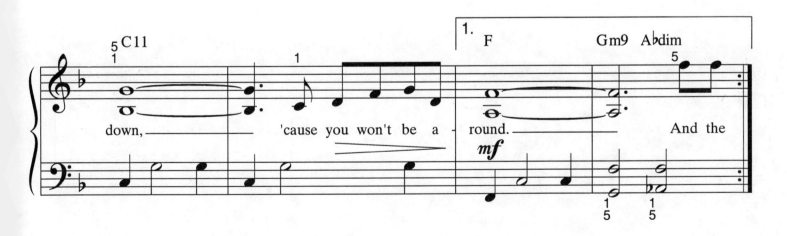

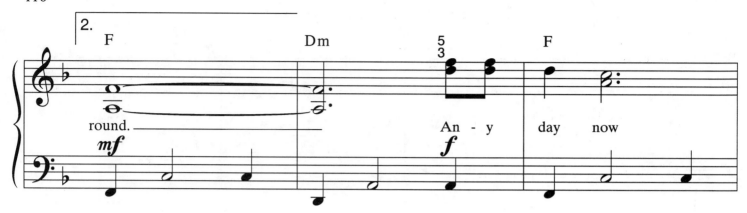

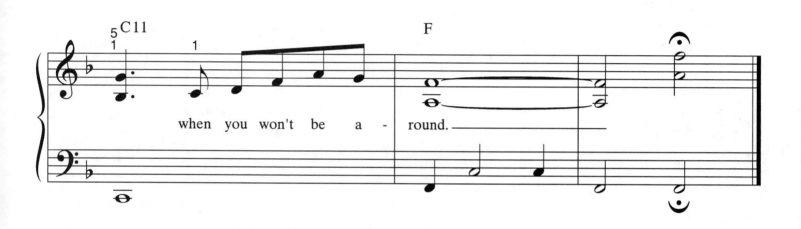

Verse 2:
Any day now
When your restless eyes meet someone new,
Oh to my sad surprise.
And the blue shadows will fall all over town, oh.
Any day now
Love will let me down, oh.

I Still Believe in You

Recorded by Vince Gill

Words and Music by
VINCE GILL and JOHN BARLOW JARVIS
Arranged by Richard Bradley

Moderately slow ♩ = 86

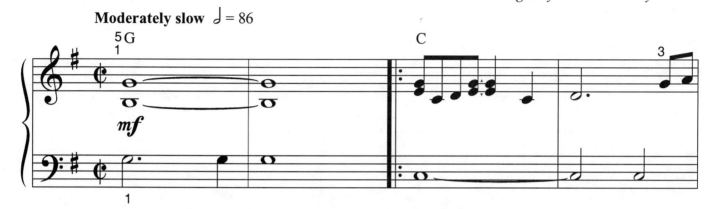

Ev-'ry-bod-y wants_____ a lit-tle piece of my time,_____

but still I put you at the

I Still Believe in You - 5 - 1

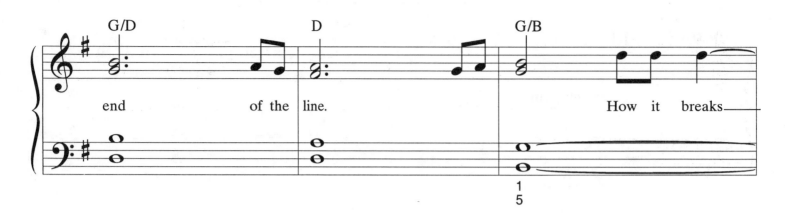

end of the line. How it breaks

— my heart to cause you this pain,

to see the tears you cry— fall-ing like rain.

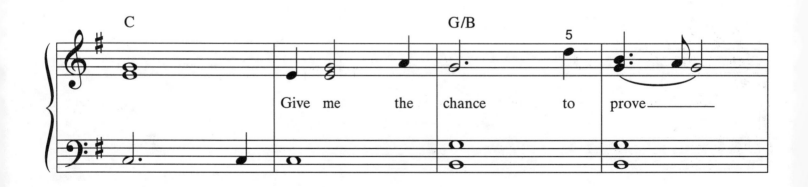

Give me the chance to prove

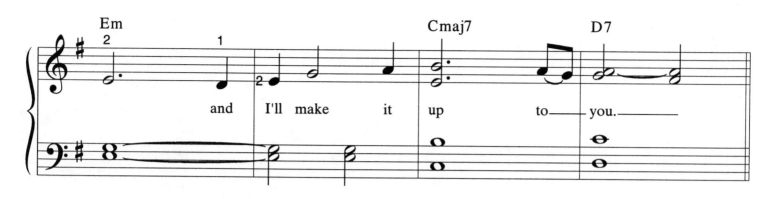

and I'll make it up to you.

I still be - lieve in you, with a

love that will al - ways be.

Stand - ing so strong and true, ba - by,

I Still Believe in You - 5 - 3

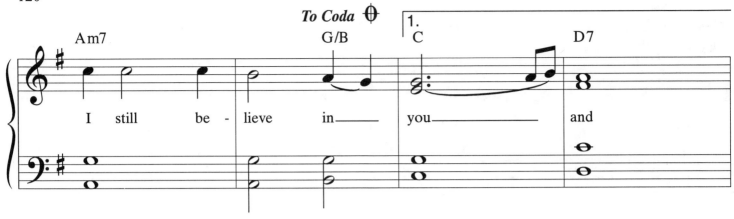

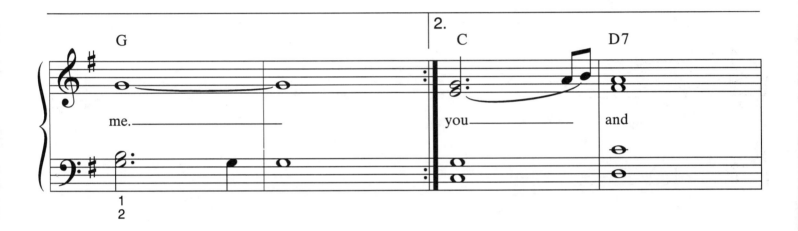

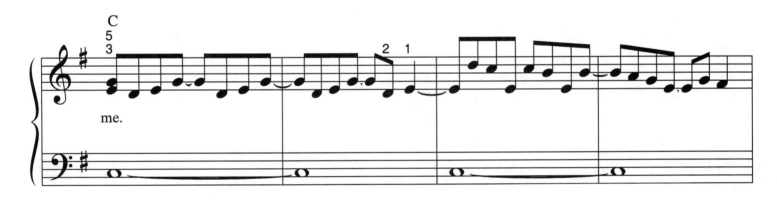

Coda

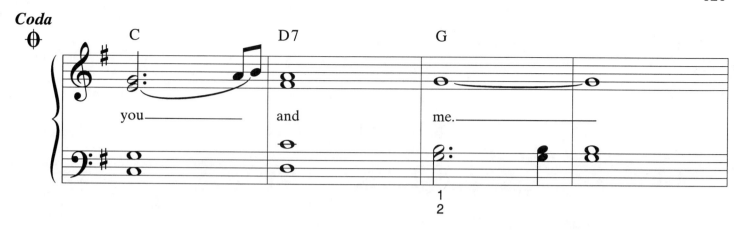

you_____ and me._____

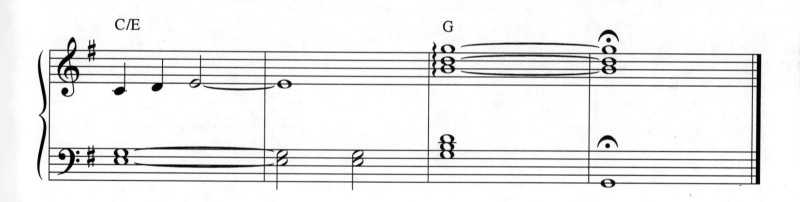

Verse 2:
Somewhere along the way, I guess I just lost track,
Only thinkin' of myself, never lookin' back.
For all the times I've hurt you, I apologize,
I'm sorry it took so long to finally realize.
Give me the chance to prove
That nothing's worth losing you.

One Friend

Recorded by Dan Seals

Words and Music by
DAN SEALS
Arranged by Richard Bradley

One Friend - 4 - 1

123

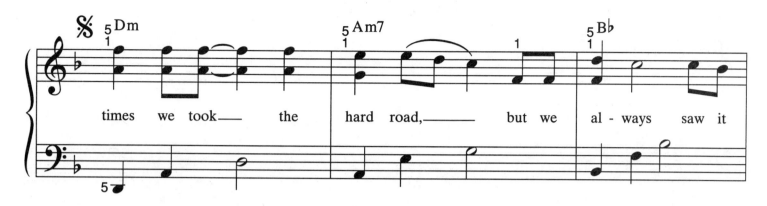

times we took—— the   hard road,—— but we   al - ways   saw it

through.——   If   I   had   on - ly   one friend left,   I

want it to—— be   you.   2. Some

you.——   Some - one   who   un - der -

One Friend - 4 - 2

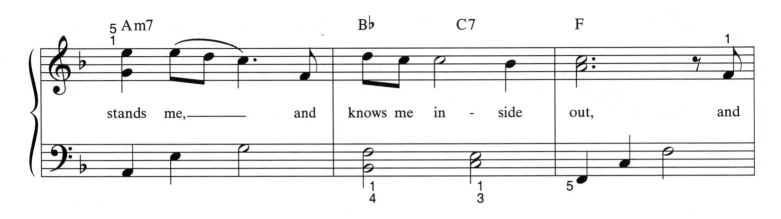

stands me,_____ and knows me in - side out, and

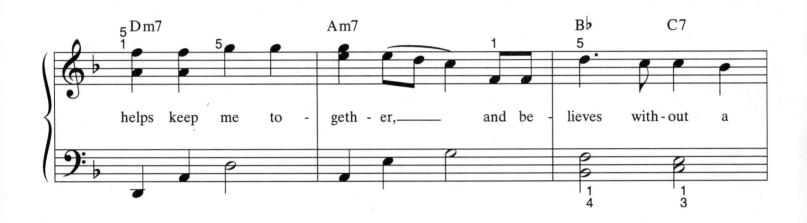

helps keep me to - geth - er,_____ and be - lieves with - out a

doubt that I could move____ a moun - tain..._____ some -

one to tell it to..._____ If I had on - ly one friend left, I'd

Verse 2:
Sometimes the world was on our side;
Sometimes it wasn't fair.
Sometimes it gave a helping hand;
Sometimes we didn't care.
'Cause when we were together,
It made the dream come true.
If I had only one friend left,
I want it to be you.

One Friend - 4 - 4

The Vows Go Unbroken
(Always True to You)

Recorded by Kenny Rogers

Words and Music by
GARY BURR and ERIC KAZ
Arranged by Richard Bradley

128

Verse 3:
Though I have been tempted,
Oh I have never strayed.
I'd die before I'd damage
This union we have made.
(To Chorus:)

The Dance

Recorded by Garth Brooks

Words and Music by
TONY ARATA
Arranged by Richard Bradley

The Dance - 4 - 1

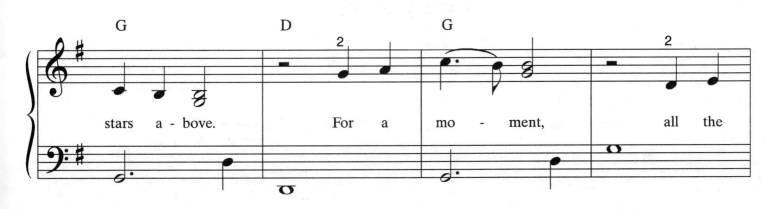

stars a - bove. For a mo - ment, all the

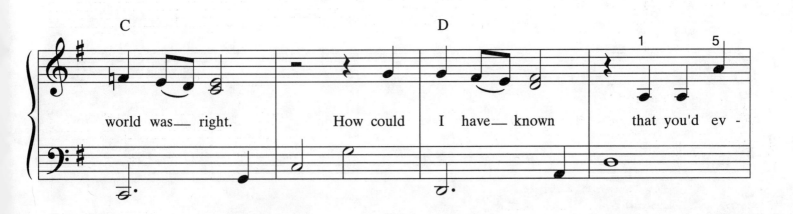

world was— right. How could I have— known that you'd ev -

er say good - bye? And now, I'm glad I did - n't

know the way it all would end,— the way it all would

132

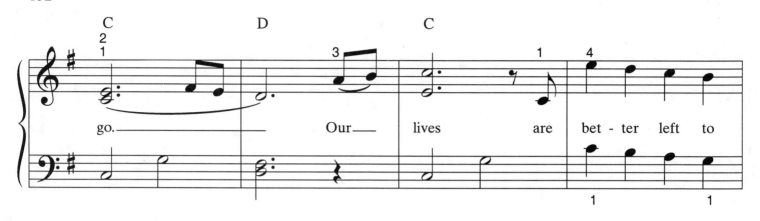

go._____ Our____ lives are bet - ter left to

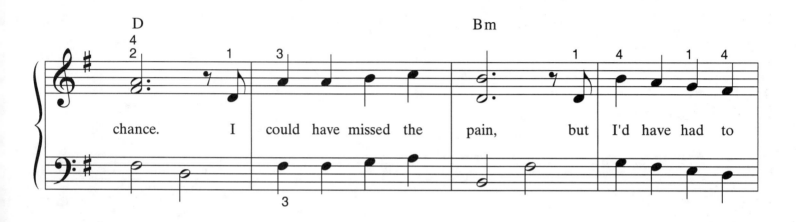

chance. I could have missed the pain, but I'd have had to

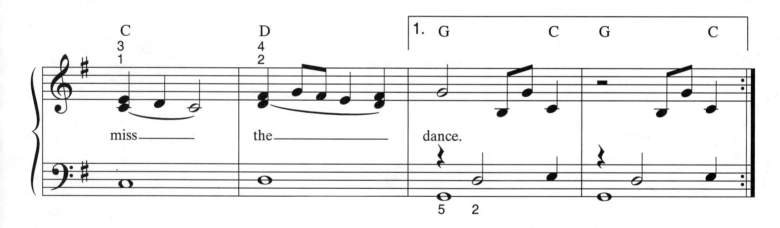

miss_____ the_____ dance.

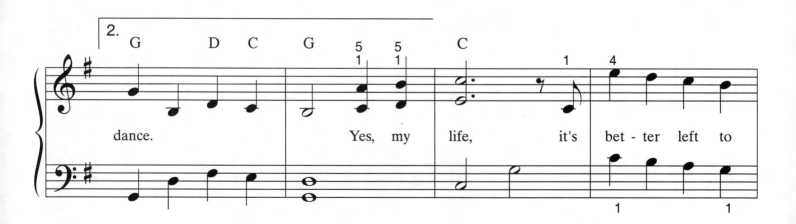

dance. Yes, my life, it's bet - ter left to

Verse 2:
Holding you, I held everything.
For a moment, wasn't I the king?
If I'd only known how the king would fall.
Hey, who's to say?
You know I might have changed it all.

I Do

Recorded by Paul Brandt

Words and Music by
PAUL BRANDT
Arranged by Richard Bradley

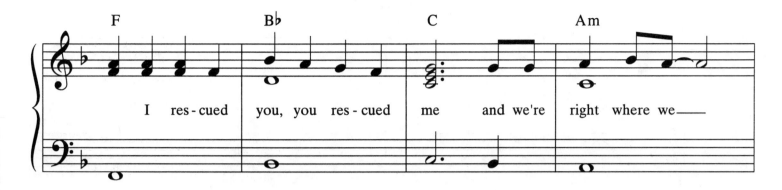

I res-cued you, you res-cued me and we're right where we——

should be when we're—— to - geth-er.

2. I know the ques-tions in your—— mind,——

but go a-head and ask me one more—— time.

138

Verse 3:
I know the time will disappear,
But this love we're building on will always be here.
No way that this is sinking sand,
On this solid rock we'll stand forever. . .
(To Chorus:)

That's the Way

Recorded by Jo Dee Messina

Words and Music by
HOLLY LAMAR and ANNIE ROBOFF
Arranged by Richard Bradley

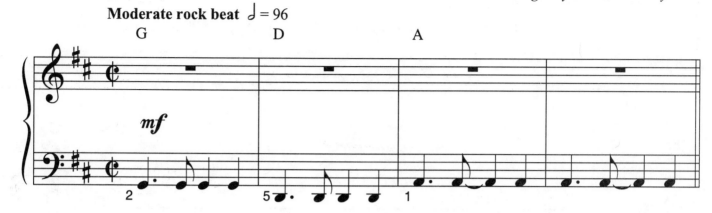

That's the Way - 5 - 1

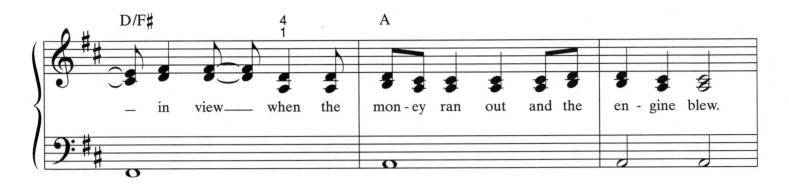

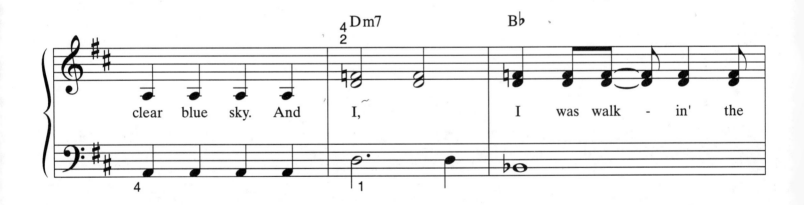

Verse 2:
One fine day you wake up, completely hopelessly fallin' in love.
He's just what you're lookin' for; the only problem is that the man's not not sure.
Another guy'll give you everything; only problem is, you don't feel a thing.
Well, I know from experience, nothing's ever gonna make perfect sense.
Oh, one day you get what you want, but it's not what you think.
Then you get what you need.

I Will Always Love You

Recorded by Dolly Parton & Vince Gill

Words and Music by
DOLLY PARTON
Arranged by Richard Bradley

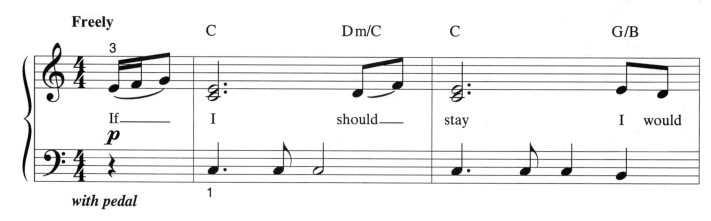

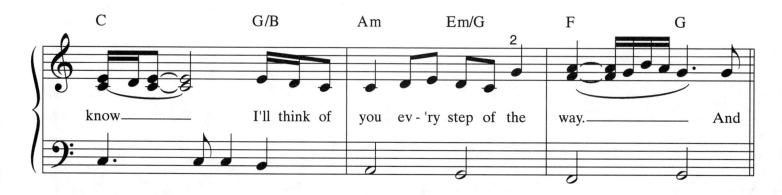

I Will Always Love You - 4 - 1

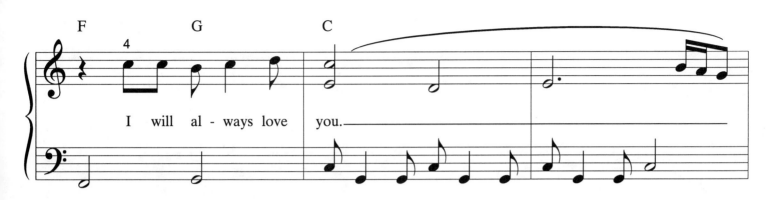

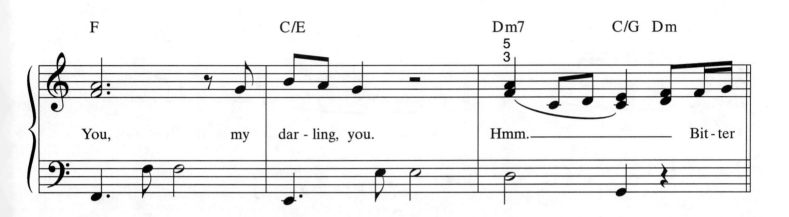

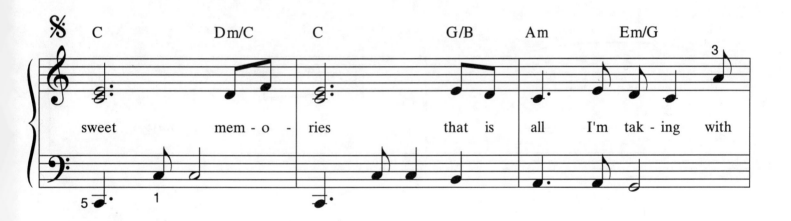

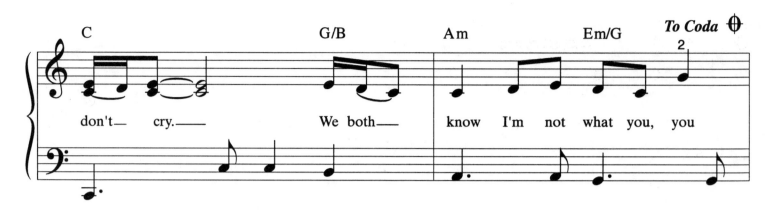

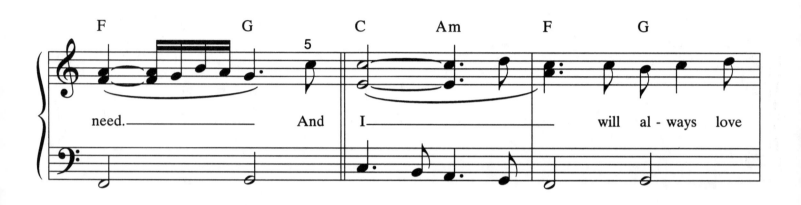

147

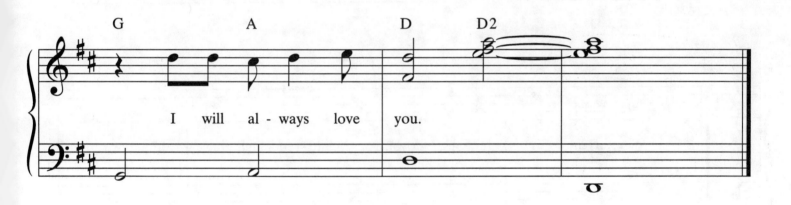

Verse 3:
I hope life treats you kind
And I hope you have all you've dreamed of.
And I wish to you, joy and happiness.
But above all this, I wish you love.

The Gift

Recorded by Jim Brickman
featuring Collin Raye and Susan Ashton

Words and Music by
JIM BRICKMAN and TOM DOUGLAS
Arranged by Richard Bradley

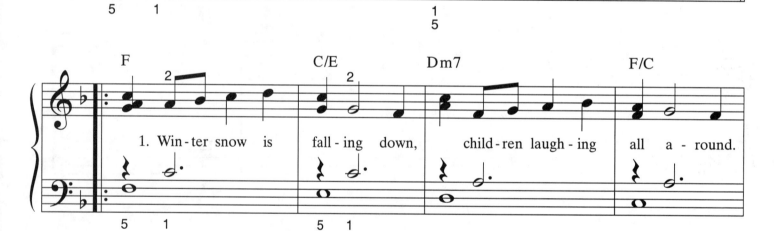

1. Win-ter snow is fall-ing down, child-ren laugh-ing all a-round.

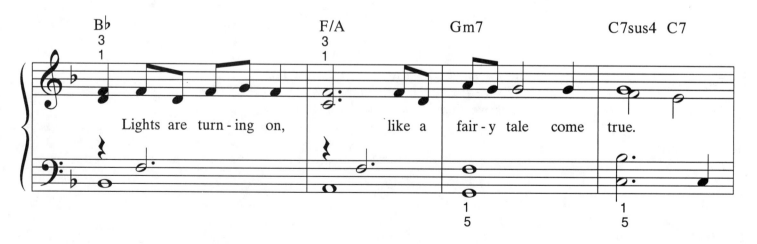

Lights are turn-ing on, like a fair-y tale come true.

The Gift - 4 - 1

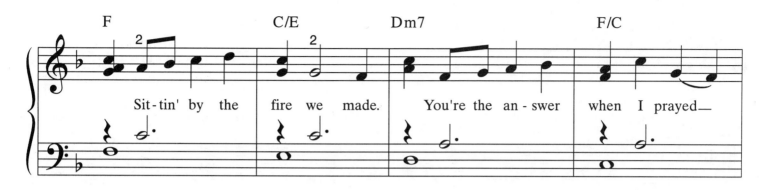

Sit-tin' by the fire we made. You're the an-swer when I prayed—

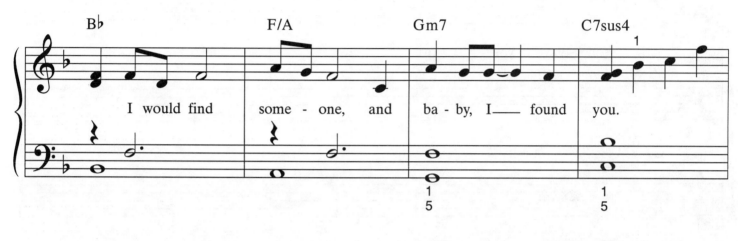

I would find some-one, and ba-by, I— found you.

And all I want is to hold— you for - ev - er.—

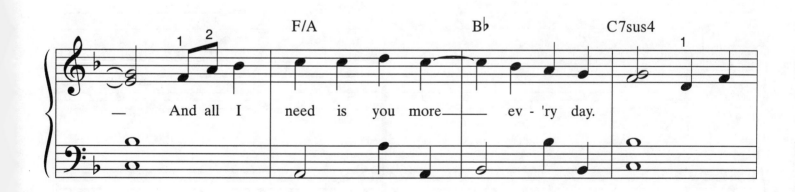

— And all I need is you more— ev - 'ry day.

The Gift - 4 - 2

150

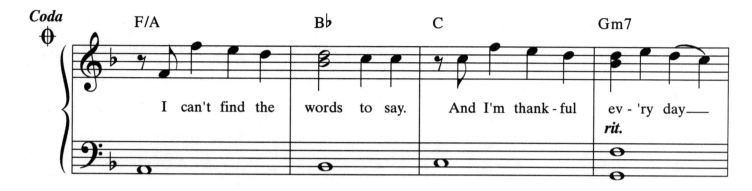

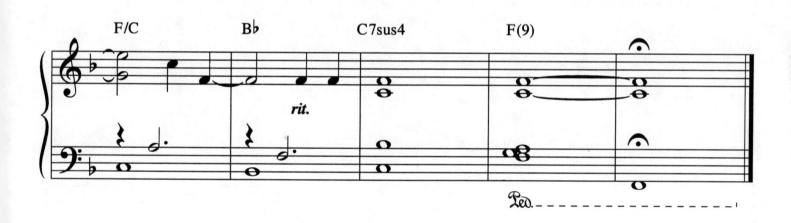

Verse 2:
Watching as you softly sleep.
What I'd give if I could keep just this moment.
If only time stood still.
But the colors fade away
And the years will make us gray.
But baby, in my eyes you'll still be beautiful.
(Chorus:)

The Gift - 4 - 4

I Cross My Heart

From the Warner Bros. Film *Pure Country*
Recorded by George Strait

Words and Music by
STEVE DORFF and ERIC KAZ
Arranged by Richard Bradley

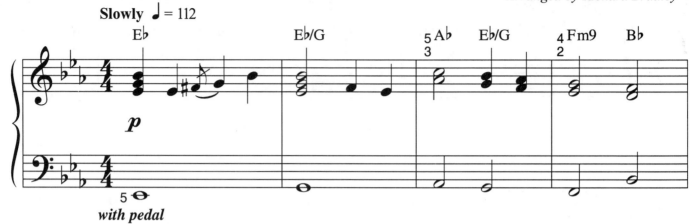

with pedal

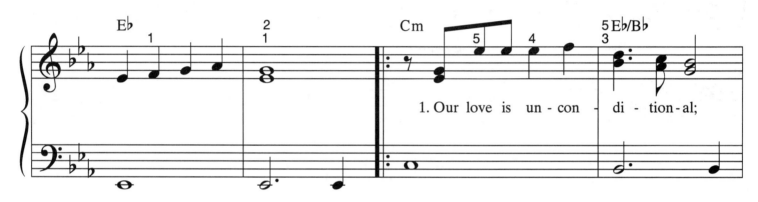

1. Our love is un-con - di - tion-al;

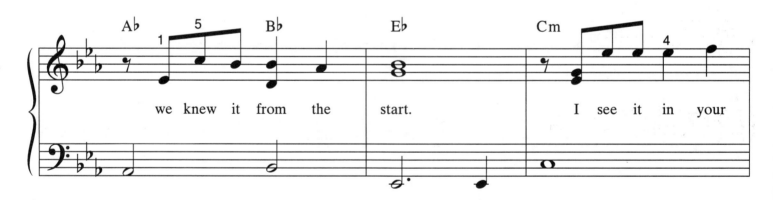

we knew it from the start. I see it in your

eyes;———— you can feel it from—— my heart.

I Cross My Heart - 4 - 1

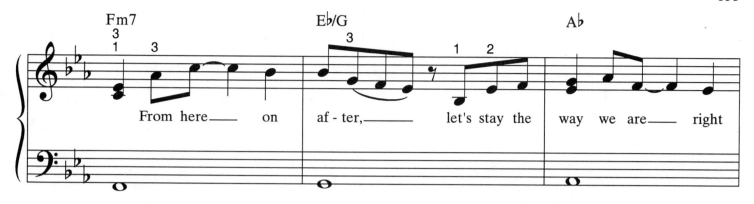

From here —— on af - ter, —— let's stay the way we are —— right

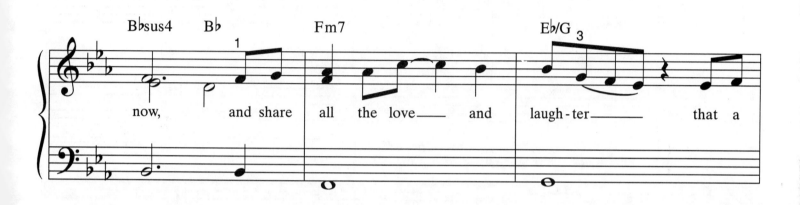

now, and share all the love —— and laugh - ter —— that a

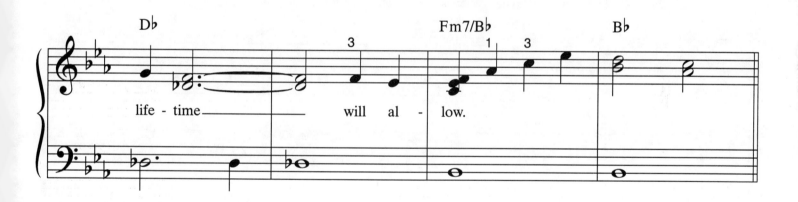

life - time —— will al - low.

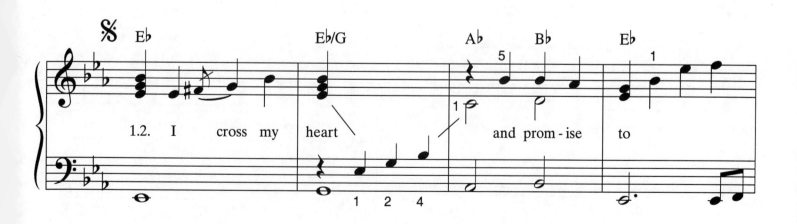

1.2. I cross my heart and prom - ise to

154

give all I've got to give to make all your dreams come true.

In all the world, you'll nev - er find

a love as true as mine.

And if a - long the way, we find a day

2. You will

mine.

Verse 2:
You will always be the miracle that makes my life complete;
And as long as there's a breath in me, I'll make yours just as sweet.
As we look into the future, it's as far as we can see,
So let's make each tomorrow be the best that it can be,
(To Chorus:)

The Chain of Love

Recorded by Clay Walker

Music and Lyrics by
JONNIE BARNETT and RORY LEE
Arranged by Richard Bradley

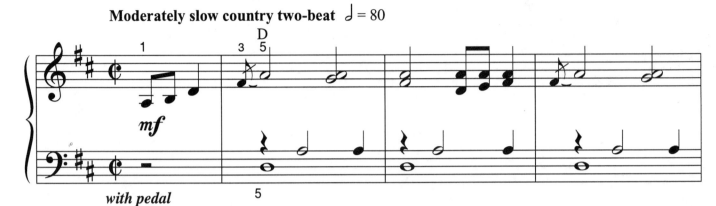

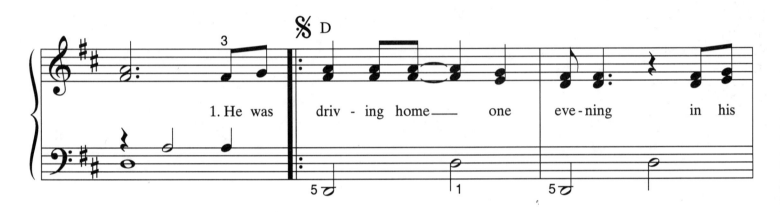

The Chain of Love - 5 - 1

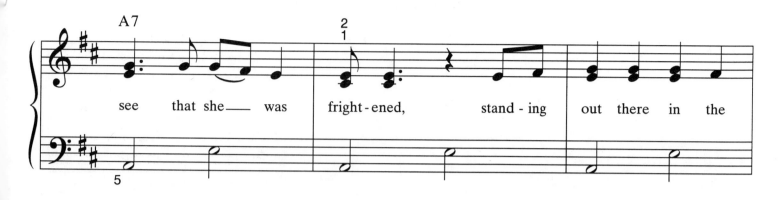

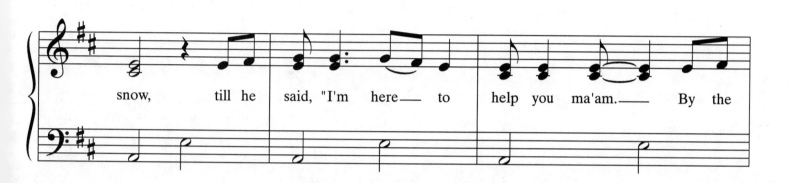

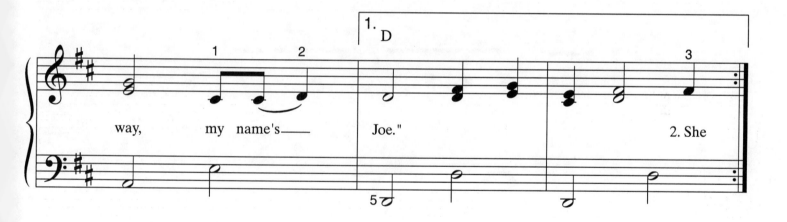

The Chain of Love - 5 - 2

158

Chorus:

thing._____ I've been there too._____ Some - one

once helped me out just the way I'm help - ing you_

— If you real - ly want to pay___ me back,___

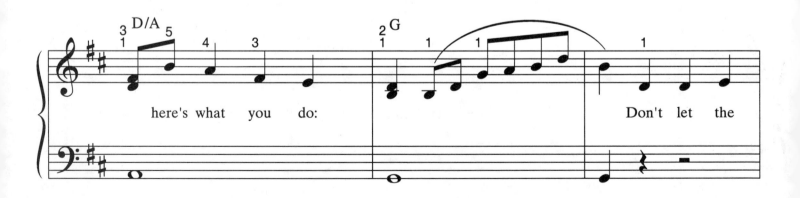

here's what you do: Don't let the

The Chain of Love - 5 - 3

chain of love_____ end with you." ___

1. | 2.
D.S. %
3. Well, a 5. That night when she___ got
mp

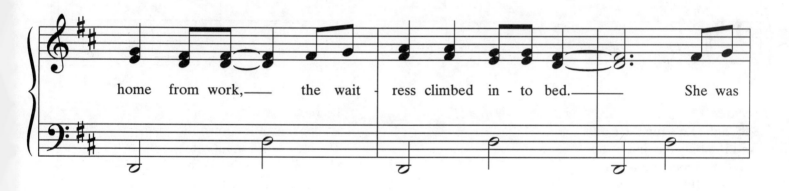

home from work,___ the wait - ress climbed in - to bed._____ She was

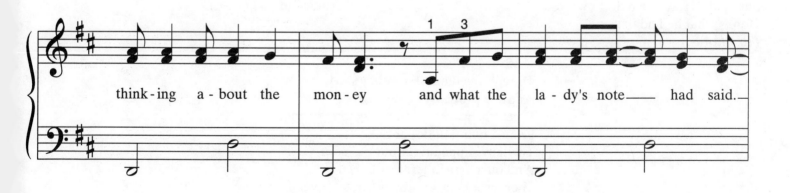

think-ing a-bout the mon-ey and what the la-dy's note___ had said._

As her hus-band lay there sleep-ing,——— she whis-pered—— soft—— and low, "Ev-'ry-thing's gon-na be al-right.—— I love you,—— Joe."——

rit.

Verse 2:
She said, "I'm from St. Louis,
And I'm only passing through.
I must've seen a hundred cars go by.
This is awful nice of you."
When he'd changed the tire
And closed the trunk,
And was about to drive away,
She said, "How much do I owe you?"
Here's what he had to say:
(To Chorus:)

Verse 3:
Well, a few miles down the road,
The lady saw a small cafe.
She went in to grab a bite to eat
And then be on her way.
But she couldn't help but notice
How the waitress smiled so sweet,
And how she must've been eight months along
And dead on her feet.

Verse 4:
Though she didn't know her story
And she probably never will,
When the waitress went to get her change
From a hundred dollar bill,
The lady slipped right out the door
And on a napkin left a note.
There were tears in the waitress's eyes
When she read what she wrote:
(To Chorus:)